This book donated
from the collection of

Tome Kurtzman
(1952-2010)

A Slice of Santa Barbara

California Riviera Cuisine

Junior League of Santa Barbara, Inc.
229 East Victoria Street
Santa Barbara, California 93101

• • •

A Slice of Santa Barbara

Published by;
Junior League of Santa Barbara, Inc.
229 E. Victoria Street
Santa Barbara, CA 93101

Printed and bound in the U.S.A. Second Edition.

ISBN 0-89951-084-1

Cover and chapter art by Henry Lenny, A.I.A.
Cover and chapter headings designed by K. Hubbard Design, Santa Barbara
Typography by Keith Messinger, *Partners Imaging Services*

Junior League of Santa Barbara, Inc.
Past & Present Cookbook Committee Members

Beverly Borneman - Co-Chair
Judy Egenolf - Chairperson
Barbara Kelly - Chairperson
Jonatha Kentro - Chair/Advisor
Mary Millikin - Chairperson
Peggy Stevens - Co-Chair

Mindy Bingham - Advisor
Rose Hodge - Advisor
Barbara Luton - Advisor
Debbie Williams - Advisor

Maureen Anderson
Amanda Bacon
Shannon Black
Lindsay Bourke
Mary Ann Burgess
Gail Campanella
Susan Carlson
Susan Devaney Corbin
Alison Crowther
Carol Fell
Erin Graffy
Leslie Granneman
Joan Harz
Lisa Keller
Le Ann Madden
Teresa Mascagno
Jennifer McKnight
Sydney Michael
Judy Milam
Laura Clarke Murphy
Anita O'berg
Ann Marie Powers
Pamela Ranstrum
Leslie Person Ryan
Adrienne Schuele
Lori Sender
Suzanne Senn
Cindy Smith
Mary Sower
Denise Spangler
Kathleen Weaver
Celia Westbury
Linda Whiston
Helene Willey
Lisa Woodworth
Jennifer Zelezny

A SLICE OF SANTA BARBARA: CALIFORNIA RIVIERA CUISINE

It is said by many who have been everywhere and could live anywhere that they choose Santa Barbara because, to them, it is paradise . . . and no wonder.

Begin with sunny, palm-lined beaches from which you can watch bobbing sailboats by day and flaming jewel-toned sunsets in the evening. The setting is framed by the rugged Santa Ynez Mountains, whose Riviera foothills are dotted with Mediterranean-style homes, their red-tiled roofs stunningly complemented by the lush foliage of scarlet bougainvillea and wild geranium.

There are the elegant estates of Montecito and the lush, green-canopied riding trails of Hope Ranch. Santa Barbara is stately in its history . . . embedded in dusty tiles unearthed from the two hundred-year-old Presidio fort; and it is dazzling in its perennial youth, flaunted by sun-bronzed surfers who gather at Rincon Point to ride the waves.

The forecast is sunny and warm year round, and seasons change so gently that they are heralded by the subtlest of clues: spring comes into full bloom along with the gorgeous purple sprays of the jacaranda trees. Summer heats up with our lively celebration of the rebirth of summer—the Summer Solstice parade up State Street, which is reminiscent of the festive Mardi gras celebration.

It catches its second wind with the sizzling excitement of August's week-long Fiesta, focusing on our Spanish and Mexican heritage, including parades, events, and the famous El Mercado food bazaars, from which emanate the luscious aromas of barbecues, chilies, cilantro, and garlic.

Autumn brings a drier, crisper touch to the ocean breezes, and the winter, warm and sunny as ever, boasts holiday lights strung on boats in the harbor and on stately palm trees. The beautiful Santa Ynez Mountains, which overlook the city, may have their peaks dusted with powdered snow.

Amidst this setting we present *A SLICE OF SANTA BARBARA*. Filled with the pleasures of the California Riviera, these recipes are inspired by the freshness of our Mediterranean climate, the tradition of our Hispanic heritage, the glamour of our star-studded community, as well as the simplicity of breakfasts on tiled terraces, beach barbecues, and picnics by our mountain streams.

For our recipes we drew upon the abundance of culinary and ethnic riches of our own regional harvest. Our groves provide avocados and citrus, while our fields grow luscious strawberries, and, for the connoisseur, kiwi and cherimoya.

There are many exotic spices in Santa Barbara's ever-popular Mexican cuisine, which are also used to flavor our local fresh snapper, shrimp, scallops and mussels, which are caught by our local fishermen.

To complete the table, perhaps a wine from one of our many fine Santa Ynez Valley vintners and, of course, a bouquet of chrysanthemums, baby's breath and statice grown in the nearby flower fields of Carpinteria.

Like life in Santa Barbara, the recipes you'll find here are easy, each tested to perfection and simple to prepare. Even if you cannot live in Santa Barbara, please be our guest for dinner, or brunch, or a Mexican fiesta, and enjoy a slice of paradise.

–Marilyn Maloney Gutsche
A Junior League member

Contents

Hors d'oeuvres

Almond-Hazelnut Stuffed Mushrooms   8
Apricots Wrapped in Bacon   23
Artichoke and Shrimp Appetizer   18
Baked Chèvre in Radicchio Cups   7
Baked Crab Appetizer   13
Balsamic Chicken Skewers   23
Bo Derek's Cheese Fondue   10
Broiled Shrimp and Chicken Skewers   19
Caviar Mousse with Crab   14
Chutney and Cheese Pâté   7
Coconut-Chicken Bites   16
Dilled Shrimp Mold   20
Escargots in Ramekins   11
Green Chili Wontons   6
Grilled Oysters with Chili-Cilantro Butter   12
Harbor Coconut Shrimp   15
Hot and Spicy Dipping Sauce   22
Hot Crab Dip   13
Layered Santa Barbara Guacamole   4
Marinated Shrimp with Orange   17
Mission Canyon Broiled Cheese with French Bread   5
Pearl Balls   22
Scallops with Sesame, Bacon, and Lime   12
Shrimp with Chèvre and Mint   15
Spinach Parmesan Puffs with Mustard Sauce   9
Stuffed Clam Bread   11
Toasted Cajun Pecans   10
Tomato-Cilantro Sauce   6
Yucatan Shrimp Fondue   21

Layered Santa Barbara Guacamole

4 ripe avocados, mashed
1/2 cup sour cream
1-2 drops Tabasco sauce
1 garlic clove, minced
1/2 teaspoon salt
1/4 cup fresh lemon juice
4 ounces sharp Cheddar cheese, grated
4 ounces Monterey Jack cheese, grated
4 medium tomatoes, diced
1/2 cup scallions, chopped
3/4 cup sliced pitted black olives
3/4 cup sour cream
1 cup salsa
1/4 cup fresh cilantro, chopped
Tortilla chips

Combine the avocados with the 1/2 cup sour cream, Tabasco, garlic, salt, and lemon juice. On a serving platter, layer ingredients in the following order: avocado mixture, cheeses, tomatoes, green onions, olives, sour cream, salsa, cilantro. Serve with tortilla chips.

Serves 8

Mission Canyon Broiled Cheese
with French Bread

4 **tablespoons olive oil**
8 **ounces Caciocavallo cheese, grated**
   (or 4 ounces Cheddar and 4 ounces Mozzarella)
2 **tablespoons fresh oregano, chopped**
   (or basil, or thyme) or 1 teaspoon dried
2 **large cloves garlic, minced**
2 **teaspoons minced parsley**
2 **tablespoons balsamic vinegar**

Turn oven on to broil. Have a rack positioned 4-6 inches below broiler element. Heat a 6-inch cast iron fry pan over medium high heat. When the pan feels hot to the touch, add the olive oil. Heat oil for 1-2 minutes, or until it looks thinned. Add the Caciocavallo to the hot oil. (It is important to add the cheese to HOT oil.) Add the oregano, garlic, parsley, and vinegar. Once the cheese is almost melted, transfer pan to preheated broiler for approximately 1 minute, or until the cheese is bubbly hot and just beginning to brown. Serve immediately with French bread slices.

Serves 4

Green Chili Wontons

1 package small wonton skins
1 pound Monterey Jack cheese
1 small can chopped green chiles

Place a 1/2 inch chunk of Jack cheese and some of the green chilies on a wonton skin. Fold up each side to make a "kiss." Wet to seal. Fry a few at a time in hot oil until golden brown. Drain and serve with tomato-cilantro sauce.

Tomato-Cilantro Sauce

2 cups fresh tomatoes, cut
2 tablespoons cilantro
1 small bunch of green onions, cut up
1 tablespoon margarine
2 cloves garlic
1/4 teaspoon paprika

Blend in blender. Put in small saucepan and bring to a boil. Reduce heat and simmer for 5 minutes. Serve warm with chili wontons.

Serves 8-12

Chutney and Cheese Pâté

3 ounces cream cheese, room temperature
1/2 cup sharp Cheddar cheese, grated
1-1/2 teaspoons dry sherry
1/2 teaspoon curry powder
Dash salt
1/4 cup mango chutney, chopped fine
3 green onions, green part only, chopped
1/2 cup cashew pieces

Beat cream cheese with mixer until light and fluffy. Mix in Cheddar cheese, sherry, curry powder, and salt. Spread the mixture in a shallow serving dish, making it 3/4 to 1-1/2 inches high. Chill 30 minutes or until ready to serve. When ready to assemble, top cheese mixture with chutney. Sprinkle chutney with chopped onions. Top with cashew pieces. Serve with assorted crackers or sliced French bread.

Baked Chèvre in Radicchio Cups

1 chèvre in log form, or Montrachet without ashes
1 teaspoon fine herbs
Oil
1 cup bread crumbs, finely grated
Radicchio

Cut chèvre into 1-inch rounds. Coat a shallow pan with oil and place cheese rounds on the pan. Coat them with oil and the herbs. Cover and refrigerate for about 1 hour. Preheat over to 400°. Remove chèvre from the oil and herb mixture and dust well with the bread crumbs. Transfer to baking sheet and bake for about 10 minutes. They should be slightly brown but firm, too much cooking and they will be runny. Place in radicchio leaves to serve.

Serves 4-6

Almond-Hazelnut Stuffed Mushrooms

1 pound large fresh mushroom caps
2 tablespoons butter
4 cloves garlic, minced
1 onion, minced
1 cup almonds, toasted well and ground
1 cup hazelnuts, toasted and ground
1 teaspoon herb salt
1 teaspoon savory herb blend (marjoram, thyme,
    basil, tarragon)
Mushroom stems, chopped and braised
2 eggs, beaten

Braise mushroom caps in butter, garlic, and onion. Mix nuts, salt, herbs, mushroom stems, and eggs. Stuff the mixture into the mushroom caps and put under broiler until browned on top.

Serves 6

Spinach Parmesan Puffs
with Mustard Sauce

For Morsels
- 2 10-ounce packages frozen spinach, thawed and squeezed dry
- 2 cups herb stuffing mix, crushed fine
- 1 cup Parmesan cheese, grated
- 1/2 cup butter or margarine, melted and cooled
- 4 small green onions, finely chopped including tops
- 3 eggs, lightly beaten

Mix all ingredients thoroughly. Shape into 1-inch balls. Place on ungreased cookie sheet leaving 1/2 inch space between each. Bake at 350° for 10-15 minutes. Serve warm with mustard sauce.

For Mustard Sauce
- 1/2 cup dry mustard
- 1/2 cup white vinegar
- 1/4 cup sugar
- 1 egg yolk

Combine the mustard and vinegar. Cover and let stand at room temperature for 4 hours. Mix sugar and egg yolk in small pan. Add mustard-vinegar mixture and cook over low heat stirring constantly until slightly thickened. Serve at room temperature.

Makes 70 Morsels

Toasted Cajun Pecans

3 tablespoons butter, melted
3 tablespoons Worcestershire sauce
1 teaspoon salt
1/2 teaspoon cinnamon
1/4 teaspoon garlic powder
1/4 teaspoon cayenne
Dash Tabasco
1 pound pecan halves

Mix above and toss with pecans. Put on baking sheet with sides and bake at 300° for 30 minutes. Stir often. Store in freezer.

Bo Derek's Cheese Fondue

2 cups white wine
4 tablespoons kirsch
1 clove garlic
1 teaspoon flour
1 pound Gruyère cheese
1 pound Emmentaler cheese
1 long loaf French bread
Pepper

Rub a heavy pot or double boiler with the garlic. Put wine, kirsch, flour, and pepper in the pot and bring to a simmer. Cube the two cheeses. Slowly add to the pot and cook over medium heat, stirring constantly. When all the cheese melts and the fondue is beginning to boil, bring it to the table and serve from a chafing dish. Dip cubed bread into the fondue.

Serves 4

Stuffed Clam Bread

1 round loaf sourdough bread, unsliced
16 ounces cream cheese
16 ounces sour cream
2 6-1/2 ounce cans minced clams, drained
1 bunch green onions, finely chopped
1 tablespoon Worcestershire sauce
Garlic, salt, and pepper, to taste

Cut a rim on the top of the loaf of bread like you would a pumpkin. Hollow out the loaf of bread with a grapefruit knife, leaving 1/2 inch thick of bread inside the crust. Mix all of the ingredients for the dip and place inside bread loaf shell. Place the top of the loaf back on as a lid. Wrap the loaf in heavy duty aluminum foil (right side up) and bake for 3 hours at 300°. Serve with cracker bread broken in medium pieces.

Serves 8-10

Escargots in Ramekins

1/2 cup celery, finely chopped
1/2 cup onions, finely chopped
1 garlic clove, minced
1 pound fresh mushrooms, sliced
4 tablespoons butter
36-48 large snails, cut in half
2 tablespoons parsley
1 egg, beaten
1 cup heavy cream
1/4 cup sherry
Salt and pepper, to taste

Sauté onion, celery, and garlic in butter for 5 minutes. Add mushrooms and cook 10-15 minutes. Remove from heat and add snails, cream, egg, parsley, sherry, salt, and pepper. Put in ramekins. Bake at 350° for 15-20 minutes.

Serves 10

Grilled Oysters with Chili-Cilantro Butter

24 Pacific oysters
1/2 pound butter
1/2 cup chiles
1/2 cup cilantro
1 lime
Cayenne

Mix together softened butter, chopped chiles, chopped cilantro, juice of one lime, and a pinch of cayenne. Place well brushed and cleaned oysters on a hot grill. When oysters pop open, pipe the chili-cilantro butter into each oyster, and serve hot.

Scallops with Sesame, Bacon, and Lime

1/2 pound large scallops, cut in half
1/2 pound bacon, cut each slice into 4 pieces
2 eggs, beaten
1/4 cup sesame seeds, toasted
4 limes, quartered

Roll each scallop in egg and then sesame seeds. Wrap with 1/4 piece of bacon and secure with toothpick. Place on broiler pan. Repeat process until all scallops are prepared. Broil 4-6 minutes turning frequently, until bacon is done. Remove from broiler. Pass lime quarters. Squeeze lime onto each piece just before eating.

Makes 20-25 pieces

Hot Crab Dip

1-1/2 cups crab meat (approximately 6 legs)
2 tablespoons lemon juice
Salt and pepper, to taste
1 cup mayonnaise
6 ounces Swiss cheese, grated
1 small onion, grated
1 tablespoon horseradish
1 teaspoon curry powder

Preheat oven to 350°. Mix all ingredients in order listed. Place in small casserole and bake for 30 minutes in 350° oven. Serve immediately with assorted crackers or sliced French bread.

Serves 4

Baked Crab Appetizer

1 green pepper, diced
2 2-ounce jars pimiento
1 tablespoon Dijon mustard
1 teaspoon salt
1/2 teaspoon white pepper
2 eggs
1 cup mayonnaise
2 pounds crab meat

Mix green pepper and pimiento. Add mustard, salt, pepper, eggs, and mayonnaise. Mix well. Add crab meat and mix with fingers. Heap on large scallop shells or small ramekins and top with a little mayonnaise. Sprinkle with paprika. Bake at 350° for 15 minutes. Serve hot or cold.

Serves 4-6

Caviar Mousse with Crab

1-1/2 envelopes unflavored gelatin
2 tablespoons cold water
1/2 cup boiling water
1 tablespoon tarragon vinegar
4 tablespoons mayonnaise
2 tablespoons fresh-squeezed lemon juice
1/4 teaspoon dry mustard
4 ounces caviar (lumpfish variety, red or black)
1 cup whipping cream

Soak gelatin in cold water to soften and then add the boiling water stirring well to dissolve. Add vinegar, mayonnaise, lemon juice, and mustard. Rinse caviar well. Drain well in strainer. Pat very dry with paper towels. Add to gelatin mixture. Whip cream to stiff peaks and fold carefully into caviar mixture. Transfer into 1-quart ring mold. Chill at least 1 hour or overnight. When ready to serve, set in hot water for 2-5 minutes being careful not to let the water touch the mousse. Turn out onto a platter and fill center with the following mixture.

---

1 cup mayonnaise
1/2 cup whipping cream, whipped to stiff peaks
1 small onion, puréed
12 ounces crab meat, cut into small pieces
1 teaspoon lemon juice
Salt and pepper, to taste

Combine all ingredients well. Serve with crackers or melba toast.

Serves 20

Shrimp with Chèvre and Mint

1 pound fresh shrimp, cleaned and cooked
1 cup olive oil
1/2 cup fresh mint, thinly sliced
3 ounces chèvre or feta cheese, crumbled
Salt and freshly ground pepper, to taste

Chill shrimp. Just prior to serving, combine with olive oil, chèvre, and fresh mint. Season to taste with salt and pepper. Serve with slices of French bread.

Harbor Coconut Shrimp

1 pound medium peeled and deveined shrimp
1/4 teaspoon salt
1/4 teaspoon ground mace
1/4 pound butter
Juice of one lime
1 large egg, well beaten
1 cup flour
1-1/2 cups grated, unsweetened coconut

Sprinkle shrimp with salt, mace, and lime juice and let stand in refrigerator for 30 minutes. Beat the egg, adding 1 tablespoon water. Dip the shrimp in flour, then egg, then coconut. Pan fry in the melted butter at low heat until golden brown on both sides about 6-8 minutes.

Serves 4-8

Coconut-Chicken Bites

3-1/2 cups sweetened shredded coconut
2 teaspoons ground cumin
3/4 teaspoon ground coriander
1/2 teaspoon cayenne
Salt and pepper
2 pounds chicken breasts, boned, skinned,
   cut in 1 inch pieces
2 eggs, beaten to blend
Dijon mustard

Preheat oven to 325°. Spread coconut on baking sheet and bake about 15 minutes or until golden brown, stirring occasionally. Transfer to bowl and cool. Coarsely grind by pulsing in processor. Butter two large baking sheets. Mix cumin, coriander, salt, pepper, and cayenne in a large bowl. Add chicken pieces and toss to coat. Add eggs and toss well. Dredge in coconut to completely coat. Arrange on baking sheets and refrigerate 1 hour to overnight. Preheat oven to 400°. Bake chicken until crisp and golden, turning once, about 12 minutes. Arrange on platter with Dijon mustard for dipping. Serve warm.

Makes about 20

Marinated Shrimp with Orange

3 **pounds large shrimp, uncooked, shelled**
4 **oranges, peeled, sectioned**
2 **red onions, sliced**
1 **cup oil**
1-1/2 **cups vinegar**
2/3 **cup lemon juice**
1/2 **cup ketchup**
1/4 **cup sugar**
1/4 **teaspoon pepper**
2 **teaspoons capers**
2 **teaspoons cilantro**
2 **teaspoons salt**
2 **teaspoons mustard seed**
1 **teaspoon celery seeds**
2 **cloves garlic, crushed**
Romaine lettuce

Cook shrimp 2 minutes in boiling water. Drain and rinse in cold water. In a large bowl, combine shrimp, oranges, and onion. Mix remaining ingredients, except lettuce, and pour over shrimp mix. Cover and refrigerate overnight or at least 8 hours. Serve in shells or on a leaf of lettuce.

Serves 12

Artichoke and Shrimp Appetizer

1 **egg yolk**
3/4 **cup olive oil**
1/4 **cup wine vinegar**
2 **tablespoons Dijon mustard**
1 **shallot, chopped fine, or 2 tablespoons onion, minced**
2 **tablespoons parsley, chopped fine**
2 **tablespoons chives, chopped**
1 **package frozen artichoke hearts, cooked**
1 **pound medium shrimp, cooked and cleaned**

Place egg yolk in blender and blend for 10 seconds. Add oil, vinegar, and mustard. Blend only until mixture is creamy. Place dressing in a bowl with shallots, herbs, artichoke hearts, and shrimp. Marinate for a few hours or overnight. Serve on a bed of lettuce.

Serves 6

Broiled Shrimp and Chicken Skewers

1 jalapeño pepper, cored, seeded, and minced
2 tablespoons shallot, minced, plus 1 large shallot, sliced
1/4 cup fresh parsley, chopped
Rind of 1/2 lemon, minced
2 cloves garlic, minced
1 tablespoon olive oil
12 large shrimp, peeled, deveined, and cut into 3
   pieces each
1/2 pound skinless, boneless chicken breast,
   cut into 1/2-inch strips
Juice of 1 lemon

Mix together jalapeño pepper, minced shallot, parsley, lemon rind, and garlic. Add the olive oil to make a fine paste. Put it in a bowl with the shrimp, chicken, and lemon juice. Let marinate for 1 hour. Heat a broiler or grill until hot. Wrap a strip of chicken around the outside of a piece of shrimp. Stick a skewer through them so both are secure. Wrap the remaining chicken and shrimp in the same way. Cook on the hot broiler or grill for 2 minutes on each side.

Yield 36

Dilled Shrimp Mold

3/4 cup Snappy Tom tomato juice
1 envelope unflavored gelatin
1-1/2 teaspoons dill weed
1/2 teaspoon salt
Few drops Tabasco
1 tablespoon lemon juice
2 tablespoons onion, grated
1/2 cup sour cream
1 cup avocado puree (2 avocados)
1/2 pound small shrimp

Pour juice in saucepan, sprinkle with gelatin and let stand 5 minutes. Stir over moderate heat until gelatin is dissolved. Remove from heat and let cool and become syrupy. Add dill, salt, Tabasco, lemon juice, grated onion, sour cream, and avocados and blend. Purée shrimp and add to avocado mixture. Pour into 3 cup mold. Refrigerate until set. Garnish with additional shrimp, cucumber, and radishes.

Serves 12

Yucatan Shrimp Fondue

1 large onion, finely chopped
2 large tomatoes, chopped
1/4 teaspoon ground cinnamon
4-6 small jalapeño chiles, seeded and finely chopped
2 pounds semisoft mild cheese
   (Jack, Teleme, Fontina, or Queso Asadero)
12 ounces tiny cooked shrimp
1-1/2 tablespoons olive oil
Salt
Tortilla chips

Heat oil in a wide frying pan over medium-high heat. Add onion and cook, stirring often, until tender (about 5 minutes). Add tomatoes and cinnamon and increase heat to high. Cook, stirring, just until liquid has evaporated (about 2 minutes). Stir in chiles, season to taste with salt. Cut cheese into 1/2 inch thick slices. In an 8-10 inch wide, 2-inch deep heatproof dish or metal pan, overlap cheese slices to cover dish bottom and extend up sides just to rim. Spoon salsa over center of cheese to make about a 6-inch circle; top with shrimp. Place dish on a grill 4-6 inches above a partial bed with medium coals. Let cheese melt; to be sure it isn't scorching on the bottom, check by pushing tip of a knife into the center of the dish. If cheese is heating too fast, move it to cooler area of grill. Serve with chips.

Serves 12-16

Pearl Balls

1 pound freshly ground pork
1/2 inch ginger, finely minced
4 scallions, finely minced
1 tablespoon dark sesame oil (not cold pressed)
1 tablespoon soy sauce
1 tablespoon cornstarch
1 teaspoon salt
1 egg white
3/4 cup glutinous (sweet) rice

Rinse rice and soak in cold water for 3-4 hours; drain. Combine all remaining ingredients. Shape into walnut-sized balls. Roll each ball in rice to completely cover. Steam over rapidly boiling water in covered steamer for one hour. Pierce each with a toothpick and remove to serving platter. Serve with hot and spicy dipping sauce.

Makes 18-25

Hot and Spicy Dipping Sauce

4 cloves garlic
1/4 teaspoon salt
1 teaspoon rice wine vinegar
1 teaspoon hot pepper oil
1/2 teaspoon sesame oil
3 tablespoons soy sauce

Peel garlic and place in mortar or heavy bowl. Add salt and mash with pestle or the handle of a heavy cleaver until mixture forms a heavy paste. Combine with remaining ingredients and mix thoroughly. NOTE: Hot pepper oil may be purchased in oriental groceries or in the oriental section of the supermarket. Hot pepper oil can be made by heating 1 cup vegetable oil until hot; remove from heat and add 2-3 tablespoons red pepper flakes; cool completely and strain. Refrigerate.

Balsamic Chicken Skewers

1-1/2 pounds boneless, skinless chicken breasts
1 tablespoon balsamic vinegar
1/3 cup white or red wine
1/2 cup chopped chutney
1/4 cup olive oil
3 peppers, green and yellow, seeded and
   cut into 1/2-inch squares or strips

Cut the chicken into 3/4-inch cubes. Put in a large mixing bowl. Add the vinegar, wine, chutney, and olive oil and stir to combine. Marinate for at least 4 hours, or overnight. Drain the chicken and put on skewers 6 inches long, alternating two pieces of chicken with pieces of yellow or green peppers. Broil or grill over hot coals for 8-10 minutes. Serve hot. Variation: Chicken can also be skewered with apple chunks, scallions, pineapple chunks, whole mushrooms, or pieces of celery.

Serves 20

Apricots Wrapped in Bacon

12 slices bacon, low sodium
24 dried apricots
3/4 cup soy sauce, low sodium
1/4 cup brown sugar
1 teaspoon ground ginger

Partially cook the bacon. Cut it in halves and wrap around a folded-in-half apricot. Secure it with a toothpick and bake at 350° on a cookie sheet for 20 minutes. Drain on paper towels. Mix soy sauce and brown sugar and ginger. Serve sauce in bowl for dipping.

Serves 12

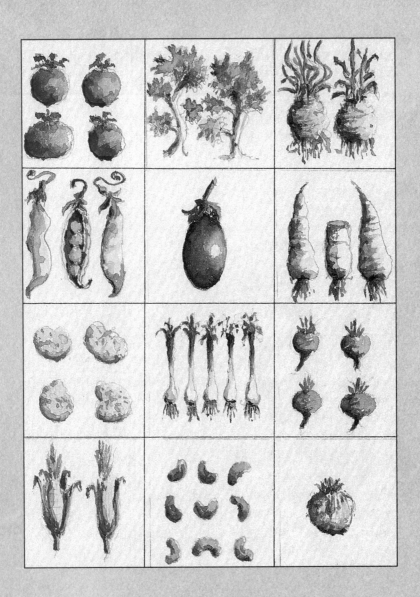

Soups

Carrot Vichyssoise   31
Chicken Bisque   36
Cioppino   27
Cold Blueberry Soup   28
Cold Cucumber Dill Soup   30
Cream of Chicken and Mushroom Soup   35
Cream of Spinach Soup   26
Cream of Tomato and Sorrel Soup   30
Curried Broccoli and Cheddar Soup   37
Curried Cold Asparagus Soup   29
Egg Roll Cartwheel Soup   42
Four Star Gazpacho   41
Mushroom Caraway Soup   43
Pea Soup au Champagne   28
Potato Leek Soup   33
Sherried Wild Rice Soup   38
Shrimp Jambalaya Soup   32
Sopa Azteca   39
Soup à L'Oignon, Chez Charlie   44
Tomato, Basil, Orange Soup   45
Tortilla Soup   40
Vegetarian Mosaic Minestrone   34

Cream of Spinach Soup

1/4 cup butter
2 packages (10 ounces each) frozen spinach
1/2 cup green onion, chopped
1/2 teaspoon rosemary
1/4 cup flour
2 cans (10-1/2 ounces each) chicken broth
1-1/2 cups water
1 medium potato
1 teaspoon salt
1/2 cup milk
1 cup cream

Defrost spinach and drain. Sauté in butter with green onions and rosemary 5 minutes. Stir in flour and gradually add broth, water. Peel and chop potato. Add to mix with salt. Simmer 20 minutes. Blend in batches until smooth. Add milk and cream.

May be served cold or hot.

Serves 6

Cioppino
(Fish Stew)

1/2 cup olive oil
3 cloves garlic, pressed
3 onions, chopped
3 carrots, peeled and chopped
2 potatoes, peeled and chopped
1/4 cup parsley, chopped
1 32-ounce can tomatoes
1 8-ounce can tomato sauce
1 cup dry red wine
1 teaspoon salt
1/4 teaspoon pepper
1/2 teaspoon paprika
1 teaspoon dry basil
Fish - 5 pounds assorted fish and shell fish

Cut fresh fish in 1-inch pieces. Clean shells of shrimp, crab, and/or lobster. Scrub and de-beard clams and mussels. Use whatever fish is seasonal. Be sure and balance strong fish with milder ones. Ask the butcher for suggestions if you are in doubt. In Dutch oven or larger kettle, sauté garlic, onions, carrots, potatoes, and parsley in hot oil. Add tomatoes, tomato sauce, wine, and seasonings. Simmer 1 hour. (May be prepared to this point 48 hours before serving. Store in refrigerator.) Warm sauce and add cut fish. Cook over low heat until fish is done (no more than 25 minutes). Add shellfish. Once shellfish open, remove from heat and serve.

Serves 6-8

Pea Soup au Champagne

20 ounces fresh frozen peas
10 ounce can chicken broth
1 pint heavy cream
Salt to taste
Dash of sugar to taste
1 small bottle champagne

In saucepan bring chicken broth to boil. Add peas and cook 3-5 minutes. Put mixture in blender or food processor and purée. Strain through fine sieve. Pour back into pan. Add cream. Season to taste. Bring just to boil. Fill small bowls 3/4 full. Add 1 teaspoon of champagne to top of soup at the table.

Serves 4-6

Cold Blueberry Soup

2 cups blueberries (fresh or frozen)
2 cups water
1/2 cup sugar
1 cinnamon stick
2 tablespoons lemon juice
2 cups plain yogurt

Boil together first five ingredients until blueberries are soft (about 10 minutes). Cool slightly, process in blender until smooth, add yogurt, mix well, chill.

Serves 6 as first course

Curried Cold Asparagus Soup

1 **pound asparagus**
5 **cups chicken broth, fresh if possible**
Salt to taste
1/4 **cup sweet butter**
1/4 **cup flour**
2 **teaspoons curry powder**
3/4 **cup heavy cream**
3 **egg yolks**
1 **teaspoon lemon juice**
Pepper, freshly ground if possible, to taste

Remove woody stem of asparagus stalk. Clean stalk with vegetable peeler. Cut off tips and save. In pot combine chicken broth and asparagus stalk, cook to boil, cover and simmer for 40 minutes. In another pot drop asparagus tips in boiling water. Cook 3 minutes or until tender. Drain and reserve the tips. Purée the stock and asparagus mixture in blender or food processor. In heavy bottom pan melt butter, add flour while stirring, 2 minutes, without browning. Add purée all at once and boil. Cook over low heat until thickened and lightly coats spoon. Stir in curry, cream, egg yolks, and lemon juice, salt and pepper to taste. Stir in asparagus tips. Chill and serve cold.

Serves 4-6

Cold Cucumber Dill Soup

2 medium cucumbers, peeled, seeded, and chopped
1 small onion, chopped
2-1/2 cups sour cream
13 ounces cream cheese
1 tablespoon lemon juice
2 teaspoons fresh dill, minced
Salt and pepper to taste

Combine all ingredients in one large bowl. Purée in the blender a few cupfuls at a time. Chill. Garnish with fresh chopped parsley or chives.

Serves 4-6

Cream of Tomato and Sorrel Soup

4 leeks (white part only), chopped
1 medium onion, chopped
3 tablespoons butter
4-5 medium baking potatoes, peeled and chopped
3 cups chicken stock
2 teaspoons salt
1/2 cup sorrel (or spinach if not available)
1 tablespoon butter
1 cup tomato juice
1 cup milk
1 cup heavy cream
3-4 tablespoons chives, snipped

In heavy saucepan sauté leek and onion in butter until soft. Add potatoes and chicken stock, bring to a boil, reduce heat and simmer for 30-40 minutes. Measure 1/2 cup shredded sorrel and cook in 1 tablespoon butter. Set aside. Purée soup in food processor. Return to pot and add sorrel, tomato juice, and milk. Bring to a simmer and adjust seasoning. Stir in heavy cream and serve either hot or very cold, sprinkled with the chives.

Serves 6-8

Carrot Vichyssoise

4 large carrots, peeled and cut into pieces
1 medium onion, peeled and cut into 4 pieces
2 potatoes, peeled and cut into 4 pieces
4 cups chicken broth
2 cups heavy cream
1 teaspoon salt
1/2 teaspoon white pepper
1/8 teaspoon cayenne
Several fresh mint leaves

Place carrots, onions, and potatoes in food processor and process until vegetables are finely diced. Put vegetables in large heavy Dutch oven. Add chicken broth and salt. Bring to a boil and cook over medium heat 25 minutes. Drain vegetables and pour broth into a large bowl. Return vegetables to processor and purée until smooth. Add vegetables to broth. Whisk in cream and stir well to mix. Add pepper. Taste to adjust seasoning. Chill well, serve with minced fresh mint leaves sprinkled on top.

Serves 6-8

Shrimp Jambalaya Soup

1 tablespoon butter
1 large onion, finely chopped
1 tablespoon flour
2 bay leaves, crushed
1/4 teaspoon ground thyme
2 tablespoons parsley, chopped
1/4 teaspoon black pepper
2 cloves garlic, crushed
1 teaspoon salt
3 tomatoes, cubed
1/2 teaspoon chili powder
1/8 teaspoon cayenne
1-1/2 quarts (6 cups) chicken broth
3/4 cup long grain rice, uncooked
1-1/2 cups shrimp, cooked, fresh, frozen, or canned

In large pot sauté onion in the butter until lightly browned. Add the flour, bay leaves, parsley, thyme, and pepper, mixing well. Rub together the salt and garlic and then add to above. Sauté about 5 minutes more but do not brown. Add the tomatoes, chili powder, cayenne and simmer 10 minutes. Add the broth and the rice and bring to a boil. Cover and simmer 30-45 minutes or until rice is barely tender, stirring occasionally. Add shrimp and heat through.

Serves 6-8

Potato Leek Soup

3 medium leeks, soaked and well cleaned
6 tablespoons butter
5 potatoes
2 medium carrots, peeled
1/2 teaspoon salt
1 bay leaf
1/4 teaspoon dill weed
1 teaspoon caraway seeds
8 cups stock (chicken, beef, or vegetable)
6 slices French bread

Chop the leeks, melt 3 tablespoons of butter in fry pan. Add leeks and sauté until golden. Cube the potatoes and carrots. Place leeks, potatoes, carrots, salt, bay leaf (whole), dill, and caraway seeds in a large pot. Pour stock into pot. Cook until potatoes and carrots are tender (approximately 20-25 minutes). Use the remaining butter on fresh bread. Toast in oven then place one piece in each soup bowl. Ladle soup over and serve immediately.

Serves 6

Vegetarian Mosaic Minestrone

1-1/2 cup dry beans (red, kidney, white, pinto,
    any kind or combination)
2 large carrots
2 zucchini
2 small onions
2 small potatoes
1 medium bunch broccoli
2 large stalks of celery
1 large can of tomatoes
1/3 cup olive oil
1/2 teaspoon sweet basil
1/2 teaspoon oregano
1/2 teaspoon dried parsley
1 cup small shell macaroni
8 cups water (6 cold, 2 boiling)
1 cup Parmesan cheese (freshly grated)

Cook the beans in 6 cups of cold water on low heat for 2 hours or until tender. Drain off liquid and save. Take 1/2 of the cooked beans and place in a blender or processor and purée. Set aside the puréed beans and the other half of beans for later use. Coarsely chop the carrots, zucchini, broccoli, potatoes, onions, and celery. In large saucepan heat 1/3 cup olive oil and sauté chopped vegetables for 5 minutes. Add tomatoes, breaking into smaller chunks, and all the liquid from the tomatoes. Add puréed beans and cooking liquid from beans (do not add whole beans at this time). Add basil, oregano, parsley, and 2 cups boiling water. Cook soup for one hour at low heat. In a separate pan boil enough water to cook the 1 cup of macaroni. When done, drain and add to the soup along with the last half of the cooked beans. Cook for another 10 minutes to allow soup to heat. Serve with fresh grated Parmesan cheese on top. It is best if left to stand in the refrigerator for 24 hours and served the next day with reheating.

Server 8-10

Cream of Chicken and Mushroom Soup

8 tablespoons butter
1 onion, finely chopped
1 pound mushrooms, sliced
5 tablespoons flour
5 cups chicken broth
1/2 cup sherry (dry)
1/2 cup half and half
1/2 cup white wine
1/2 teaspoon hot pepper sauce
5 chicken breasts, cooked, boned, and diced
1/4 teaspoon tarragon

Cook 5 boned, skinned chicken breasts in white wine, 6 cups water and 1/2 onion in 350° oven for 45 minutes. When cool, cut into bite-sized chunks and use chicken stock to make 5 cups of broth. In large kettle, melt 3 tablespoons of butter over medium-low heat. Sauté onions and set aside, then sauté mushrooms. Set aside. Melt 5 tablespoons of butter and gradually add 5 tablespoons of flour; stir continually and allow roux to blend. Add heated chicken broth gradually, stirring until well mixed. Add sherry, half-and-half, hot pepper sauce, chicken, mushrooms, onion, and tarragon.

Serves 4-6

Chicken Bisque

3 tablespoons butter
1/2 cup julienne carrots
1/4 cup green onions
1/4 cup flour
1 teaspoon salt
Dash nutmeg
Dash white pepper
1 10-ounce can chicken broth
1/4 cup cognac or brandy
1-1/2 cups cooked chicken, chopped
1-1/2 cups heavy cream

Sauté carrots and onion in butter, stir in flour, salt, nutmeg, and pepper. Slowly add broth, brandy, or cognac. Bring to boil. Cook and stir over low heat until thickened. Add 1-1/2 cups heavy cream and chicken. Heat through and serve.

Serves 6

Curried Broccoli and Cheddar Soup

1-1/2 pounds broccoli
1/4 cup butter or margarine
1 tablespoon curry powder
1 medium onion, chopped
6 cups chicken broth
2 large thin skinned potatoes or 3 medium, cubed
4 slender carrots, thinly sliced
1 cup milk
3 cups shredded sharp Cheddar cheese

Trim flowerettes from the broccoli and cut into small pieces. Discard the tough ends of stems. Peel stems and slice thinly. In a 6-8 quart kettle, melt butter over medium heat and add curry powder and onion. Stir for 5 minutes. Add the broth, potatoes, broccoli stems, and carrots. Cover and simmer until potatoes mash easily, about 30 minutes. Process the broth and vegetables in a processor, and return to kettle. Heat soup to boiling, add broccoli flowerettes and milk. Simmer uncovered just until the flowerettes are tender when pierced. Stir in cheese a handful at a time until melted.

Serves 6-8

Sherried Wild Rice Soup

2/3 cup raw wild rice
2 cups salted water
2 medium leeks, sliced
10-12 fresh mushrooms, sliced
1/2 cup butter
1 cup flour
8 cups hot chicken broth
Salt and pepper to taste
1 cup half-and-half
3 tablespoons dry sherry

Wash wild rice. Place in heavy saucepan with salted water. Bring to boil. Simmer covered for about 45 minutes until tender, but not mushy. Uncover, fluff with a fork. Simmer additional 5 minutes. Drain excess liquid. Sauté leeks and mushrooms in butter 3 minutes or until soft. Sprinkle in the flour, stirring and cooking until flour is cooked, but not browned. Slowly add the chicken broth, stirring until the flour mixture is blended well. Add the rice and season to taste with salt and pepper. Heat thoroughly but do not boil. Stir in half-and-half and sherry. Heat gently.

Serves 8-10

Sopa Azteca

2 whole chickens
2 medium onions, quartered
1 bunch cilantro
4 large cloves garlic
3 bay leaves
8 chili negro (black chiles)
Salt, pepper, garlic powder to taste
Water to cover
8 ounces salsa

Simmer above ingredients in a large 8-quart soup pot for 2-1/2 hours, except chiles which are added the last half hour. Add salsa last 10 minutes. Remove chiles, strain soup, bone and shred chicken. Replace chiles. Serve with following condiments.

1 large package tortilla chips
2 avocados, sliced
1 pint sour cream
1-1/2 pounds Monterey Jack cheese, cubed

To assemble, place some of the tortilla chips and Jack cheese in bowls and add the chicken and broth (very hot) and top with avocado slices and some sour cream.

Serves 6-10

Tortilla Soup

1 large onion, chopped
4 ounces diced green chiles, canned (3 if fresh)
5 cloves garlic, minced
1/4 cup olive oil
6 cups chicken stock (homemade is preferable)
2 cups beef stock (spicy homemade is preferable)
2 cups spicy tomato juice
3 tablespoons chili powder
1 tablespoon ground cumin
2 tablespoons salt
1 teaspoon pepper
1 teaspoon Worcestershire sauce
1 teaspoon prepared steak sauce
1 tomato, large, peeled, seeded, and chopped
1/2 cup cilantro, well washed, leaves only
8 corn tortillas, 6 inch
Vegetable oil (enough to fry tortilla strips)
1 ripe avocado, large
1 teaspoon lemon juice
1 pound each Cheddar cheese and Jack cheese, shredded
3 cups shredded chicken (optional)
2 cups shredded brisket (optional)

In a large kettle, sauté onion, chiles, and garlic in olive oil. Add stocks, tomato juice, chili powder, cumin, salt, pepper, steak sauces, chopped tomato, and cilantro. Mix well. Bring to boil. Reduce heat and simmer, covered for 1-1/2 hours. Meanwhile, stack the corn tortillas together and trim the sides to form a square. Cut into 1-1/2 inch long by 1/2-inch wide strips, resembling noodles. In a heavy, deep frying pan, heat oil 1 inch deep to medium heat. Fry the tortilla "noodles" 1-2 minutes, stirring constantly, until just lightly browned. Remove from oil with a slotted spoon. Drain on paper towels. Lightly salt while still warm. When cooled, store in an airtight container until ready to use. Fifteen minutes before serving, peel and cube avocado and brush with lemon juice to prevent discoloring. Divide avocado into individual bowls. Ladle hot soup over each. Serve at once. Top with cheese. Meats may be added to soup bowls for a heartier meal.

Serves 8-10

Four Star Gazpacho

8 large tomatoes, peeled, seeded, and chopped
2 green peppers
1 bunch green onions
1 red onion
2 cucumbers
4-5 garlic cloves, minced
1/2 cup olive oil
2 tablespoons salt
6 tablespoons red wine vinegar
3 slices French bread, crumbled
1 teaspoon white pepper
2 cups tomato juice
4 cups water, or as needed

Chop all vegetables. Combine garlic, olive oil, salt, wine vinegar, French bread, and pepper in deep bowl. Add vegetables. Add tomato juice and water. Refrigerate for 4-6 hours. Serve in chilled bowls.

Serves 8

Egg Roll Cartwheel Soup

6-10 egg roll sheets
Filling
1/2 pound ground pork
1 tablespoon light soy sauce
1 teaspoon sherry
1/2 teaspoon sugar
1/4 teaspoon salt
Dash black pepper
1 egg, beaten
1 tablespoon cornstarch, dissolved in 3 tablespoons water
   and 2 tablespoons sesame oil
2 cups packed fresh spinach
1 teaspoon sugar
5 cups chicken stock
Light soy sauce to taste

Chop ground pork to loosen, then put in bowl and add soy sauce, sherry, sugar, salt, and pepper; mix well. Add beaten egg in a circular motion until well blended. Then pour in dissolved cornstarch and stir until very smooth. Let sit for 10 minutes to "fluff out."

Egg Rolls: Place an egg sheet on a flat surface; give meat a few big stirs and cover sheet with 1-2 tablespoon filling, to within 3/4 inch from edge. Brush edge with half cornstarch paste, then lift the edge closest to you and roll sheet to other end. Press down all edges to seal. Place rolls, seam side down—1/2 inch apart on heatproof plate and steam over high heat for 15 minutes. Remove, drain, and refrigerate.

Spinach: Blanche in small pot of boiling water with 1 teaspoon sugar. Pinch off tough stems. Drain well.

Final Cooking: Slice egg rolls diagonally into 1/2 inch thick cartwheels. Bring stock to boil, then scatter in cartwheels, cover and simmer for about 2 minutes. Add spinach and simmer 1 minute. Season to taste with light soy sauce.

Serves 6

Mushroom Caraway Soup

1/2 pound mushrooms
3 teaspoons butter
1/2 teaspoon caraway seeds
1/2 teaspoon paprika
1 tablespoon flour
3-1/2 cups chicken stock
1 egg yolk
1 cup sour cream
2 tablespoons fresh dill (or 1-1/2 teaspoons dried dill)
Salt and pepper

Slice and sauté mushrooms in butter with caraway and paprika for 1 minute. Sprinkle with flour and blend well. Add chicken stock. Simmer covered 30 minutes. Whip egg yolk with fork until creamy; add sour cream and dill. Spoon sour cream mixture into tureen and add hot soup slowly, stirring constantly. Garnish with additional dill.

Serves 6

Soup à L'Oignon, Chez Charlie

3 tablespoons butter
1 tablespoon olive oil
8 large onions (yellow, thinly sliced)
1 teaspoon salt
1/2 teaspoon sugar
3 tablespoons flour
2 quarts hot beef bouillon
   (2 cans diluted with 4 cans of water)
1 cup white wine
1 bay leaf
1/2 teaspoon sage
3 crushed garlic cloves
Garlic melba rounds
3/4 cup cognac
1 pound grated Swiss cheese
Parmesan cheese
Curry and ground allspice

Melt the butter with the oil in the saucepan; add the sliced onions and garlic, and stir to coat with butter. Cover the pan and cook over moderately low heat for 20 minutes, stirring occasionally, until the onions are tender and translucent. Then uncover the pan, raise heat to moderately high, and stir in the salt and sugar. Cook for 30 minutes, stirring frequently, until onions have turned an even, deep golden brown. Then lower heat to moderate, stir in the flour, and add a bit more butter if the flour does not absorb into a paste with onions. Cook slowly for 2 minutes stirring, to brown flour lightly. Remove from heat.

Pour in about a cup of the hot bouillon, stirring with a wire whip to blend flour and bouillon. Add the rest of the bouillon and the wine, bay, sage, and garlic and bring to simmer. Add dash of curry, ground allspice, and salt and pepper to taste. Simmer slowly for 40 minutes (For best results, prepare the night before, cool, and keep covered in refrigerator overnight.)

Before serving, add cognac and bring the soup to boil. Use ladle to fill individual serving bowls to within 1/2 inch of the top. Sprinkle Swiss cheese over soup to form a light layer of cheese. Place the garlic rounds in a closely packed layer over the cheese. Mix some Parmesan cheese with the Swiss cheese. Sprinkle cheese mixture to completely cover the garlic rounds with a thick layer of cheese. Sprinkle a tablespoon of oil over the cheese. Bake in the middle level of preheated 350° oven for 15 minutes or until the soup is bubbling slowly and cheese has melted. Meanwhile, heat your broiler to high; just before serving, run the soup under the hot broiler for a moment to brown the cheese lightly. Cover the bowls with lids and serve steaming hot.

Serves 8-10

Tomato, Basil, Orange Soup

2 cups Italian-style canned tomatoes, drained
1 medium onion, sliced
2 tablespoons butter
1/2 teaspoon salt
1 garlic clove, minced
1-1/2 tablespoons fresh basil (or 1 teaspoon dried basil)
1 pinch thyme
2 cups beef bouillon
1 cup tomato juice (from tomatoes)
1/2 cup fresh orange juice
1 bay leaf
Grated orange zest and fresh basil as garnish

In a saucepan combine tomatoes, onion, butter, salt, garlic, basil, and thyme. Cover and simmer over low heat for 30 minutes. Purée in food processor and return to pan. Add rest of ingredients (except orange zest and basil) and simmer partially covered for 25-30 minutes. Serve hot or very cold and garnish with orange zest and basil.

Serves 6

Salads

Asparagus in Raspberry Vinaigrette 67
Avocado and Papaya Salad with Orange Flower Hazelnuts 66
Beef Salad with Asparagus and Broccoli 56
Bleu Cheese/Buttermilk Dressing 76
Blueberry and Chèvre Salade 69
Caesar Salad 52
Cajun Blackened Snapper and Pasta Salad 74
Cantaloupe and Avocado Salad with Bacon 63
Cantaloupe and Raspberries with Sherry 61
Chicken and Red Grape Salad 59
Chinese Chicken Salad 51
Crab and Tortellini Salad 68
Fiesta Chicken Salad Olé! 70
German Potato Salad 53
Gingered Pork Tenderloin Salad 64
Greek Salad 51
Green Beans, Artichokes, and Chèvre 60
Green Goddess Salad Dressing 76
Herbed Tomato Slices, Feta Cheese, and Pine Nuts 62
Marinated Vegetable Salad 50
Mushroom Quarters with Tarragon Cream Dressing 72
Orange Slices with Poppy Seed Dressing 55
Pasta Primavera 48
Pescado Con Papaya 73
Potato Salad with Pesto 54
Salade Napoli 57
Shrimp and Scallop Salad with Snow Peas 58
Sour Cream Dressing 77

Pasta Primavera

Pasta
  1 pound Italian fettuccini, broken into 2-inch pieces
  1/3 cup olive oil
  1/4 cup white wine vinegar
  1 tablespoon Spanish sherry wine vinegar
  Salt and freshly ground pepper

Vegetables
  16 very thin asparagus, trimmed and
      cut into 1-1/2 inch lengths
  2-3 cups broccoli flowerettes
  2-3 cups fresh peas or frozen petite peas, defrosted
  6 green onions
  1 pint small cherry tomatoes
  1 pound fresh spinach leaves

Seafood
  2 pounds bay or sea scallops
  2 pounds uncooked large shrimp
  1/3 cup olive oil
  3 tablespoons wine vinegar
  3 tablespoons Spanish sherry wine vinegar
  1 clove garlic, minced
  Salt and freshly ground pepper

Basil cream
  1/3 cup white wine vinegar
  2 tablespoons Dijon mustard
  1/2 cup tightly packed fresh basil leaves
      or 3-4 tablespoons dried basil
  1-2 garlic cloves
  1/3 cup vegetable oil
  1 cup sour cream
  1/2 cup whipping cream
  3 tablespoons minced fresh parsley
  Salt and freshly ground pepper

Pasta:

Put pasta into 8 cups boiling water. Cook to "al dente." Drain. Transfer to large bowl, add oil and vinegars and toss. Cover and refrigerate.

Vegetables:

Separately steam asparagus and broccoli just until crisp. Steam fresh peas (do not cook frozen peas). Store vegetables separately. Mince green onions and half of cherry tomatoes. Rinse spinach and chill.

Seafood:

Cut sea scallops in half, poach in water about 2 minutes. Poach shrimp in shells in same manner. Rinse all seafood. Shell and devein shrimp, cut shrimp lengthwise. Transfer seafood to another large bowl, add oil, vinegars, and garlic and toss.

Basil cream:

Combine vinegar, mustard, basil, and garlic in processor and mix until smooth. Drizzle in oil with machine running. Add sour cream, whipping cream, and parsley. Season to taste. Refrigerate.

To assemble:

About 30 minutes before serving arrange spinach leaves around platter edges. Gently toss pasta with vegetables and reserve green onion-tomato mixture. Arrange in center of platter with spinach leaves as border. Make a well in center of pasta. Drain seafood, toss with green onion-tomato mixture and mound in center of pasta. Serve with basil cream.

Serves 12

Marinated Vegetable Salad

6 zucchini
1 red onion, sliced in rings
1 medium green pepper, sliced
1 medium red pepper, sliced
3 medium tomatoes, sliced
1 16-ounce can sliced ripe olives
1/4 cup fresh parsley, finely chopped
1/4 cup red wine vinegar
2/3 cup olive oil
1 teaspoon each of oregano, basil, thyme
1 teaspoon capers
1/4 teaspoon dry mustard
2 cloves garlic, minced
Salt and pepper to taste

Parboil whole zucchini for 3 to 4 minutes. Drain and refrigerate until cold. Slice zucchini into thin diagonal slices. Put in large bowl and add remaining ingredients. Toss. Marinate for at least 3 hours in refrigerator.

Serves 6

Greek Salad

4 large red tomatoes
3 cucumbers, peeled, seeded, and sliced
4 stalks celery
1 red onion, cut into thin rings
1/4 pound feta cheese
1-1/2 teaspoons dried oregano
Dressing
1/3 cup red wine vinegar
2/3 cup olive oil
Dash salt and pepper
1/2 teaspoon oregano

Cut tomatoes into large chunks. Peel, seed and slice cucumbers into large chunks. Slice celery on diagonal. Slice onion thinly and separate rings. Crumble feta cheese and add oregano. Prepare dressing and toss.

Serves 6-8

Chinese Chicken Salad

6 whole chicken breasts, boned, cooked, and shredded
4 stalks celery, sliced on diagonal
8 green onions, sliced on the diagonal
1/4 pound bean sprouts
1 can chow mein noodles
1/2 head Savoy or Chinese cabbage,
   sliced thinly and separated
Dressing
1/3 cup rice vinegar
2/3 cup sesame oil and olive oil combined
3 tablespoons sesame seeds
1/3 cup soy sauce

Combine shredded chicken, sliced celery, green onions, and cabbage. Add bean sprouts and chow mein noodles. Toss with dressing.

Serves 6-8

Caesar Salad

1　large bunch Romaine lettuce, washed,
　　dried and chilled
3-4　cloves fresh garlic, minced
5-6　tablespoons extra virgin olive oil
2-3　tablespoons Worcestershire sauce
4-5　tablespoons freshly grated Parmesan cheese
1/2　can anchovies, finely chopped,
　　　or 2 teaspoons anchovy paste, or to taste
Juice of 1/2 fresh lemon
1　egg, coddled
Salt and freshly ground black pepper, to taste
Garlic croutons

Combine olive oil, Worcestershire sauce, minced garlic, and anchovies in a large wooden salad bowl; set aside. Just before serving, stir dressing again and add lettuce. Toss to coat, then add lemon juice and toss again. Meanwhile, bring a small saucepan of water to a boil; add egg just for a second; immediately run under COLD water. Add egg to salad and toss thoroughly again. Add Parmesan cheese, salt, pepper, and croutons; toss and serve immediately.

Serves 2-3 as main course, 4-6 as salad course

German Potato Salad

2-1/4 pounds Idaho potatoes (approximately
    7 medium potatoes)
1/4 cup fresh parsley, chopped
1/4 cup scallions, thinly sliced
1 beef bouillon cube, dissolved in 1/2 cup boiling water
1/4 cup vegetable oil (corn or safflower)
1 teaspoon salt
1/2 teaspoon freshly ground pepper
1/2 teaspoon sugar
1/4 teaspoon dill weed
2 tablespoons Dijon-style mustard
3 tablespoons white wine vinegar

Cook potatoes in simmering water until tender, approximately 20 minutes. Cool enough to handle. Peel and cut in half lengthwise. Thinly slice the halves. Place potato slices in a large mixing bowl with the parsley and the scallions. Combine the dissolved bouillon, oil, salt, pepper, sugar, dill weed, mustard, and vinegar, whisking well. Pour the dressing over the potatoes and herbs. Toss gently to coat. Cover and let stand for at least 1 hour to allow flavors to mature. Serve at room temperature.

Serves 6

NOTE: Great to take on a picnic since refrigeration is not required!

Potato Salad with Pesto

2-1/2 pounds small new potatoes
4 ounces sliced black olives
7 ounces pesto with garlic
1 cup freshly grated Parmesan cheese
1/2 cup fresh basil, shredded
Salt and pepper to taste

Boil potatoes 10-15 minutes until tender, then drain. Cut into bite-sized pieces. Add above ingredients to potatoes while still warm and toss. Salt and pepper to taste. Refrigerate before serving.

Orange Slices with Poppy Seed Dressing

Salad
- 4 large navel oranges
- 1 avocado, sliced
- 4 thin slices medium-sized red onion
- 1 head romaine lettuce

Dressing
- 1/2 cup safflower oil
- 1/4 cup ketchup
- 2 tablespoons sugar
- 1/4 teaspoon salt
- 1/8 teaspoon poppy seed
- 2 green onions

Wash the green onions and remove the root ends. Pat dry and slice thinly. Place the oil, ketchup, sugar, salt, poppy seed, and green onions into a jar with a tight-fitting lid. Shake well to blend.

Peel the oranges and remove the white membrane. Cut into thin slices. Wash the lettuce, pat dry and thinly shread. Separate the onion slices into rings. Cut a few onion rings into thirds for a garnish. Peel and slice the avocado.

Place a bed of shredded lettuce on each of four chilled salad plates. Scatter red onion rings over the lettuce and arrange a sliced orange on top. Place sliced avocado on top of orange, then a few onion strips. Drizzle generously with the dressing and serve immediately.

Serves 4

Beef Salad with Asparagus and Broccoli

Ginger dressing
>   2/3 cup light soy sauce
>   1/2 cup rice vinegar
>   6 tablespoons sesame oil
>   3 inch piece fresh ginger root, grated
>   2 teaspoons sugar
>   1/2 teaspoon freshly ground pepper

Salad
>   1-1/2 pounds flank steak
>   1 pound fresh asparagus
>   1 pound fresh broccoli
>   1 medium red onion
>   12 cherry tomatoes

Combine the light soy sauce, rice vinegar, sesame oil, grated ginger, sugar, and pepper in a container with a tight-fitting lid. Shake well to combine.

Marinate the flank steak in 3/4 cup of the ginger dressing for 20 minutes or up to several days covered tightly in your refrigerator. Barbecue or broil the steak to desired doneness. Slice the asparagus on the diagonal into 2-inch pieces. Cut the broccoli into bite-sized florets. Steam the vegetables separately over boiling water until crisp tender, 3-5 minutes. Thinly slice the red onion and separate into rings. Slice the cherry tomatoes in half. Thinly slice the beef, being sure to cut across the grain of the meat diagonally.

Combine the asparagus, broccoli, red onion rings, tomatoes, and beef and toss with enough ginger dressing to evenly coat well. Serve at room temperature.

An outstanding picnic main attraction!

Serves 4

Salade Napoli

Dressing
- 3 large cloves garlic
- 1 large green onion
- 1 cup olive oil
- 1/4 cup red wine vinegar
- 2 tablespoons fresh lemon juice
- 3 tablespoons parsley, chopped
- 3/4 teaspoon salt
- 1/2 teaspoon freshly ground pepper
- 3/4 cup freshly grated parmesan cheese

Salad
- 10 ounces thinly sliced salami
- 6 large green onions
- 1 large green pepper
- 1 pound Mozzarella cheese
- 4 large tomatoes
- 1 15-ounce can garbanzo beans
- 1 15-ounce can sliced black olives
- 2 heads Romaine lettuce

Finely mince the garlic using the metal blade in your food processor. Add the green onion and 6 tablespoons of the olive oil and process until puréed. Add the remaining olive oil, the vinegar, lemon juice, salt, pepper, and parsley. Process until well blended, approximately 30 seconds. Add the Parmesan cheese and process for 15 seconds. Chill the dressing for at least 1 hour and stir well just before pouring over salad.

Stack the salami slices and cut into julienne strips. Thinly slice the green onions. Finely dice the green pepper. Grate the Mozzarella cheese. (You should have approximately 2-1/2 cups.) Seed and chop the tomatoes. Drain the garbanzo beans and the olives well. Thinly shread the Romaine lettuce. Place the salami, green onions, green pepper, Mozzarella cheese, garbanzos, olives, and Romaine in a large bowl and toss well with the dressing. Refrigerate for 2 hours before serving.

Serves 8

Shrimp and Scallop Salad
with Snow Peas

Salad
- 2 medium cucumbers
- 4 large celery stalks
- 24 large shrimp, shelled and deveined
- 1-1/2 pounds large (Eastern) scallops
- 1/2 pound fresh snow peas, ends trimmed

Mustard dressing
- 1/3 cup rice vinegar
- 1/4 cup safflower oil
- 1/2 teaspoon salt
- 1/2 inch piece fresh ginger root, grated
- 2 tablespoons dry mustard
- 2 tablespoons sesame oil
- 3 tablespoons dry sherry
- 1 tablespoon sugar

Place the vinegar, oil, salt, grated ginger, dry mustard, sesame oil, dry sherry, and sugar in a container with a tight-fitting lid. Shake well to combine.

Peel the cucumbers and cut in half lengthwise. Trim and discard the ends. Using a spoon, scrape out the seeds, then cut into medium slices. Place in a large mixing bowl and set aside. Wash, trim, and thinly slice the celery. Add to the cucumber. Bring six cups of water to a brisk boil in each of two medium saucepans. Boil the shrimp briefly just until pink. Drain well and place in a large mixing bowl. Boil the scallops just until translucent. Drain well and add to the shrimp. Fill a tea kettle full of water and bring to a rolling boil. Place the trimmed snow peas in a colander and pour the boiling water over to crisp cook. Let drain, then add to the cucumber/celery mixture. Toss the seafood with half of the dressing. Toss the vegetables with the remaining dressing. Mound the seafood on each of four salad plates. Surround with the vegetables. Chill for 20 minutes before serving.

Serves 4

Chicken and Red Grape Salad

4 cups cooked chicken, diced
1 cup sliced celery
1 pound red flame seedless grapes, stems removed
1 10-ounce can sliced water chestnuts, well drained
1-1/2 cups slivered almonds, lightly toasted
1-1/2 cups mayonnaise
1-3 teaspoons curry powder
1 tablespoon soy sauce
1 tablespoon fresh lemon juice
2 cups fresh pineapple chunks
6 large butter lettuce leaves, well chilled

Combine the chicken, celery, grapes, water chestnuts, 1 cup of the slivered almonds, mayonnaise, curry powder (to taste), soy sauce, and lemon juice. Refrigerate overnight to allow the flavors to mature. Serve the chicken salad in lettuce cups garnished with fresh pineapple and the remaining 1/2 cup slivered almonds.

Serves 6

Green Beans, Artichokes, and Chèvre

1/3 cup fresh lemon juice
1/2 cup olive oil
3/4 pound fresh green beans
1 medium clove garlic, minced, or to taste
Salt and pepper to taste
4 dashes hot pepper sauce or to taste
10 ounces frozen artichoke hearts, defrosted
2 tablespoons butter
2 medium tomatoes
4 ounces goat cheese (Cabecou)
3 tablespoons fresh thyme leaves or 1 tablespoon dried
   romaine, or other lettuce leaves as garnish

Measure the lemon juice and olive oil and set aside. Cut the beans diagonally into 2-inch lengths and blanch in boiling salted water for 3-4 minutes, until tender crisp. Rinse well in cold water to stop the cooking process and pat dry. Toss the beans with the garlic, 2 tablespoons of the olive oil, 1 tablespoon of the lemon juice and the hot pepper sauce. Refrigerate until ready to use. Chill at least 20 minutes or up to 3 days.

In a medium-sized skillet, heat the butter until lightly browned and add the artichoke hearts. Sauté until lightly browned. Drizzle with 1 tablespoon of the lemon juice. Set aside to cool until ready to use.

Seed and coarsely chop the tomatoes. Dice the goat cheese. Toss the beans, artichoke hearts, tomatoes, goat cheese, thyme leaves, remaining lemon juice, and remaining olive oil. Serve on a bed of crisp, well-chilled lettuce leaves.

Serves 4

Note: This salad presents beautifully in a glass bowl for a buffet. Or, your favorite pasta tossed with a simple dressing, such as olive oil, minced garlic, and freshly grated Parmesan cheese, makes a nice bed for this salad when served as the main course for a luncheon.

Cantaloupe and Raspberries with Sherry

1 **pint fresh raspberries**
3 **tablespoons sugar**
1/4 **cup cream sherry**
1 **large cantaloupe**

In a blender or food processor, purée 3/4 cup of the raspberries. (Keep the remaining berries chilled.) Force the purée through a wire strainer into a small bowl to remove the seeds. Add the sugar and cream sherry to the puréed berries, combine well, cover, and refrigerate until ready to use.

Cut the cantaloupe into chunks or balls. Mix the cantaloupe with the raspberry purée and keep chilled. When ready to serve, spoon the melon mixture into sherbet or wine glasses (long stemmed preferred) and top with the remaining berries. The fruit salad can also be placed in a glass bowl and served buffet-style. The raspberry and cantaloupe color combination is lovely.

Serves 6

Herbed Tomato Slices, Feta Cheese, and Pine Nuts

10 fresh basil leaves or 2 teaspoons dried
1/4 cup fresh chives
1/4 cup fresh parsley
2 cloves garlic, minced (optional)
1 teaspoon salt
1/4 teaspoon pepper
1/2 cup olive oil
1/4 cup tarragon vinegar
4 large beefsteak tomatoes
1/2 cup pine nuts
1/2 red onion
4 ounces feta cheese

Have ready a container in which to marinate the tomatoes. Remove the stems from the basil leaves, stack them, thinly slice into shreds (julienne cut), and place in the selected container. Using scissors, thinly "snip" the chives into the container. Coarsely chop the parsley and add to the container. Add the minced garlic, salt, pepper, olive oil, and tarragon vinegar. Whisk to combine the ingredients.

Thickly slice the tomatoes so that you have three large slices for each person. Add the tomato slices to the marinade, being sure to coat both sides generously. Cover tightly and refrigerate for at least 2 hours or up to 2 days.

Place pine nuts in a single layer on a cookie sheet. Lightly toast in a 400° oven until golden. Thinly slice the red onion and separate into rings. Crumble the feta cheese.

Lay three large tomato slices on each of four chilled salad plates. Sprinkle 1/4 of the red onion rings, feta cheese, and pine nuts over each. Spoon the remaining marinade over each, being sure to include the julienned basil and serve immediately or chill for up to 30 minutes.

Serves 6

Cantaloupe and Avocado Salad
with Bacon

French dressing
   2/3 cup onion
   1 cup light vegetable oil
   2/3 cup ketchup
   1/2 cup red wine vinegar
   1/2 cup sugar
   2 teaspoons sweet paprika
   2 teaspoons salt
Salad
   1 pound bacon
   1 large cantaloupe
   2 heads Romaine lettuce
   3 large avocados

Finely mince the onion. Place the onion, vegetable oil, ketchup, red wine vinegar, sugar, paprika, and salt in a container with a tight-fitting lid. Shake well to combine.

Broil, microwave, or pan fry the bacon until well done, drain well on paper towels and crumble. Set aside. Using a melon baller, cut cantaloupe into balls. Refrigerate until ready to use. Wash the romaine lettuce and pat dry. Tear into bite-sized pieces, place in an airtight container or plastic bag with a twist tie, and refrigerate to crisp until ready to serve. Peel and dice the avocados just prior to serving.

Transfer the lettuce, avocado, melon, and bacon to a large salad bowl and toss with the French dressing. Serve immediately. A perfect accompaniment to barbecued meats.

Serves 8

Gingered Pork Tenderloin Salad

Marinade
- 4 tablespoons soy sauce
- 2 tablespoons dry sherry
- 2 cloves garlic, pressed or minced
- 1 inch ginger root, peeled and thinly sliced
- 2 tablespoons brown sugar
- 2 teaspoons sesame oil
- 2 tablespoons honey
- 1/4 teaspoon 5-spices powder
- 2 pounds pork tenderloin

Dressing
- 2 tablespoons white sesame seeds, lightly toasted
- 3 tablespoons dry sherry
- 1/4 cup rice vinegar
- 1 tablespoon Dijon mustard
- 1/2 teaspoon chili sauce (Tabasco)
- 1 tablespoon sugar
- Salt and pepper to taste
- 1/4 cup light vegetable oil

Salad
- 8 cups shredded Savoy cabbage
- 4 scallions, diagonally sliced
- 1/2 inch ginger root, peeled and finely grated
- 1/2 teaspoon salt
- 1/2 cup fresh lemon juice
- 4 tablespoons white sesame seeds, lightly toasted

Combine the soy sauce, dry sherry, garlic, sliced ginger root, brown sugar, sesame oil, honey, and 5-spices powder in a container suitable for marinating the pork tenderloin. Add the well-trimmed meat to the marinade, cover well, and let the flavors mature overnight in refrigerator.

To seal in the juices, place the marinated meat into a preheated 500° oven for 10 minutes. Lower the oven temperature to 350° and finish cooking the pork, brushing often with the juices and marinade that collect in the pan, approximately 15-20 minutes. Juices should run clear when meat is pierced.

Slice the pork across the grain into bite-sized pieces. Toss lightly with any marinade remaining in the pan.

Place sesame seeds, rice vinegar, mustard, chile sauce, salt, pepper, and oil in a food processor or blender and blend until smooth.

Place the cabbage, garlic, scallions, puréed ginger root, salt, and lemon juice into a large bowl. Massage the mixture with your hands until the squeaky noise of the cabbage is gone.

Drain any excess juices from the pork, then toss with the cabbage. Serve in individual bowls garnished with the toasted sesame seeds. Chopsticks are a nice touch.

Serves 8

Note: To turn this salad into a main course, double the dressing ingredients. Prepare thin Chinese noodles and toss with enough dressing to coat. Slice a variety of vegetables such as cucumber, celery, avocado, radishes, carrots, snow peas, tomatoes, etc. Place the noodles in the center of each plate topped with the pork tenderloin salad. Arrange the sliced vegetables around the outside of the noodles and drizzle with dressing.

Avocado and Papaya Salad
with Orange Flower Hazelnut Dressing

Dressing
- 3 heaping tablespoons lightly toasted hazelnuts
- 2 tablespoons orange flower honey
- 2 tablespoons white wine vinegar
- 2 teaspoons Dijon mustard
- 2 tablespoons finely chopped orange zest
- 1/4 teaspoon salt (or to taste) freshly ground pepper to taste
- 1/2 cup light vegetable oil

Salad
- 2 ripe avocados
- 1 ripe papaya
- 1 head butter lettuce
- 4 teaspoons coarsely chopped hazelnuts, lightly toasted

Place three heaping tablespoons hazelnuts in a blender or food processor and process until finely ground. Add the orange flower honey, wine vinegar, mustard, orange rind, salt, and pepper. Process for a few seconds to combine. With the motor running, slowly drizzle in the oil.

Wash the lettuce and pat dry. Peel and slice the avocados and papaya. Place a bed of lettuce on four chilled salad plates and top with the avocado and papaya slices arranged into a fan shape. Drizzle with the dressing and sprinkle each salad with 1 teaspoon hazelnuts. Serve immediately.

Serves 4

Asparagus in Raspberry Vinaigrette

30 spinach leaves, washed and chilled
30 asparagus spears, trimmed to 4-5 inches,
   cooked and chilled
1 10-ounce package frozen raspberries in syrup, drained
6 tablespoons virgin olive oil
1/4 cup whipping cream
2 tablespoons sherry vinegar
Salt and pepper
1 teaspoon chopped chives
Cracked black pepper

Steam asparagus spears until tender. Chill. Purée raspberries in food processor. Strain and discard seeds. Combine next four ingredients in processor and mix well. To serve, place five spinach leaves on salad plates; arrange five asparagus spears on top. Spoon ribbon of vinaigrette over center. Garnish with chives and pepper.

Serves 6

Crab and Tortellini Salad

Dressing
- 2 egg yolks
- 1/4 cup tarragon vinegar
- 1/4 cup fresh lime juice
- 1-1/2 tablespoons Dijon mustard
- 1 tablespoon chopped fresh tarragon or 1 teaspoon dried
- 1 teaspoon crushed fennel seeds
- 2 large cloves garlic, pressed or minced
- 1/2 teaspoon salt or to taste
- Freshly ground pepper to taste
- 2/3 cup extra virgin olive oil

Salad
- 1 pound fresh tortellini
- 2 bunches spinach
- 1/2 medium red onion
- 1 green bell pepper
- 1 red bell pepper
- 2 medium tomatoes
- 1-1/2 cups sliced black olives
- 1 pound fresh crab (or substitute)

Lightly whisk the egg yolks, then add the vinegar, lime juice, mustard, tarragon, fennel seeds, garlic, salt, and pepper. Whisk to combine well. Continue whisking as you slowly pour in the olive oil. Refrigerate until ready to use. Cook tortellini to desired doneness, rinse in cold water, and drain well. Toss the tortellini with 1/4 cup of the salad dressing and set aside. Wash the spinach, discard the tough stems and dry the leaves. Place the spinach in an airtight container (or plastic bag) in the refrigerator to crisp. Thinly slice the red onion and separate into rings. Cut the red and the green bell peppers into thin strips (julienne cut). Coarsely chop the tomatoes. Drain the olives. Using your fingers, pull crab apart into small, bite-sized pieces and remove any shell or cartilage pieces.

Combine all ingredients in a large salad bowl and toss with enough dressing to coat well. Can be chilled briefly prior to serving (no more than 30 minutes), or served immediately. This is a lovely summer brunch main course.

Serves 6

Blueberry and Chèvre Salade

Dressing
- 1 egg
- 2 tablespoons red wine vinegar
- 1/4 cup fresh blueberries
- 1/4 cup safflower oil
- 1/4 teaspoon Dijon mustard
- 1/4 teaspoon salt
- Fresh pepper to taste
- 1 tablespoon poppy seeds

Salad
- 2 heads butter lettuce
- 1 pint (less 1/4 cup) fresh blueberries
- 8 ounces chèvre

Place the egg, vinegar, 1/4 cup blueberries, Dijon mustard, salt, and pepper in a food processor or blender. Process until well blended, approximately 1 minute. With motor running, drizzle the oil slowly into the dressing. When all of the oil is used, the dressing should be creamy and thickened. Add the poppy seeds and use an on/off motion to distribute evenly. The dressing can be used immediately or refrigerated for up to 2 days.

Wash the lettuce and pat dry. Place the dry leaves in an airtight container or plastic bag securely twist-tied and put in the refrigerator to crisp until ready to use, Rinse and drain the blueberries and keep chilled, Crumble the chèvre.

Toss the lettuce with just enough dressing to thinly coat. Divide the lettuce evenly onto four chilled salad plates, Sprinkle each with 1/4 of the chèvre and 1/4 of the blueberries. Drizzle with any remaining dressing.

Serves 4

Fiesta Chicken Salad Olé!

Chicken salad
- 1 bunch cilantro (approximately 1 cup)
- 1/2 bunch parsley (approximately 1 cup)
- 2 fresh jalapeño chiles
- 1 large white onion
- 2 large cloves garlic
- 1 cup dry white wine
- 4 tablespoons ground cinnamon
- 1 teaspoon salt
- 1/4 teaspoon cayenne
- 3 whole large chicken breasts
- 4 large stalks celery
- 6 large radishes
- 1 cup sour cream

Salsa fresca
- 3 large cloves garlic
- 2 large fresh tomatoes
- 1 28-ounce can whole Italian plum tomatoes
- 1 medium onion
- 3 large stalks celery
- 1 medium green bell pepper
- 3 large fresh green chiles (or 7 ounce can)
- 4 tablespoons fresh cilantro leaves
- 1/2 teaspoon salt or to taste
- 1/8 teaspoon pepper or to taste

Garnish
- 12 6-inch corn tortillas
- Pure vegetable oil for frying
- 1 head iceberg lettuce
- 1-1/2 cups grated Cheddar cheese
- 1 cup sour cream
- 3 medium tomatoes
- 3 avocados
- 1 lime, quartered and seeded
- 18 cilantro leaves

In a large casserole, combine cilantro (stems and all), parsley (stems and all), chiles with stems and seeds removed, quartered white onion, quartered garlic cloves, wine, cinnamon, salt, and pepper. Toss chicken breasts in the mixture, cover and bring to a boil over medium-high heat.

Lower heat and simmer for 12-15 minutes, until cooked throughout. Check to be sure meat next to bone is no longer pink. Remove chicken and set aside until cool. Strain the chicken stock and reserve. When chicken is cool enough to handle, discard skin and bones and, using your fingers, shred the meat into bite-sized pieces. Toss the chicken with 1/4 cup reserved stock and set aside.

Slice the celery and the radishes. Add to the chicken and toss the mixture with the sour cream. If more moisture is needed, use the reserved chicken stock sparingly. Keep the salad chilled until ready to use. (The leftover stock should be reserved for other uses.)

Purée the garlic in a food processor. Coarsely chop the fresh tomatoes, canned tomatoes (well drained), onion, celery, bell pepper, and green chiles separately in the processor, using an on/off motion and emptying each into one large mixing bowl as ready. Add the cilantro leaves, salt and pepper to taste and combine well. Taste for seasoning. Cover well and chill. Pour off any excess liquid just prior to using.

Stack the tortillas and cut into 1/4-inch x 2-inch noodles. Add 1-inch of oil to a heavy deep fry pan. Heat the oil to approximately 375°. Fry the noodles in small batches for 1-2 minutes, stirring constantly until just lightly browned. Remove from oil using a slotted spoon and let drain on paper towels. Lightly salt while still warm. Thinly shred the iceberg lettuce. Seed and coarsely chop the tomatoes. Peel and coarsely chop the avocados and drizzle with lime juice.

Place a bed of tortilla noodles on each of six plates. Place shredded lettuce over tortillas. Place a mound of chicken salad in the center and top with shredded cheese, tomatoes, avocado, salsa fresca and a dollop of sour cream. Garnish top with three cilantro leaves. This better-than-classic tostada can also be served in a "Make-Your-Own-Buffet Style."

Serves 6

Mushroom Quarters with Tarragon Cream Dressing

Dressing
- 2 tablespoons mayonnaise
- 2 tablespoons white wine vinegar
- 1 tablespoon fresh lemon juice
- 1 clove garlic, pressed or minced
- 1/2 teaspoon dry mustard
- 1/2 teaspoon dried tarragon (1-1/2 tablespoons fresh)
- 1/2 teaspoon salt (or to taste)
- 1/4 teaspoon freshly ground pepper
- 1/4 teaspoon sugar
- 1/2 cup extra virgin olive oil, or other good quality vegetable oil

Salad
- 3/4 pound fresh mushroom caps
- 3 cups shredded daikon radish
- 1 red bell pepper, julienned
- 2 tablespoons capers, rinsed and drained

Place the mayonnaise, wine vinegar, lemon juice, garlic, dry mustard tarragon, salt, and pepper in a blender or food processor and process for 4 seconds. With the machine running, slowly add the oil. The dressing will be thick and creamy. Use immediately or store in refrigerator for up to 3 days.

Toss the mushrooms in the dressing. Place 1/4 of the shredded daikon radish on each of four chilled salad plates. Arrange the julienned red pepper around the outside of the daikon. Mound 1/4 of the mushrooms in the center of each plate. Sprinkle each salad with 1/2 tablespoon capers.

Serves 4

Pescado Con Papaya
Sole with Papaya

1 firm-ripe papaya (1 to 1-1/2 pounds)
4 fillets Petrale sole (6 to 8 ounces each)
5 tablespoons fresh lime juice
1/4 teaspoon salt
1/3 cup flour
4 tablespoons butter
1 tablespoon light vegetable oil
1/8 teaspoon ground cinnamon
1 tablespoon brown sugar

Cut the papaya in half lengthwise. Scoop out and discard the seeds. Using a sharp paring knife, remove the skin from the papaya and cut lengthwise into 1/3-inch slices. Set aside.

Sprinkle the fish with 2 tablespoons of the lime juice, let stand for 5 minutes, then lightly sprinkle the fillets with salt. Dip each into the flour to coat on both sides, shaking off the excess.

In a large skillet over medium-high heat, melt 2 tablespoons of the butter in the oil. When the butter becomes foamy, add the fish in batches and sauté, turning once, until golden brown, approximately 1-1/2 to 2 minutes per side. Remove fish to a serving platter and keep warm in a 200° oven.

Add the remaining 2 tablespoons butter to the skillet. Heat until bubbly, then add the papaya slices. Sprinkle with cinnamon. Sauté, turning very gently, about 1 minute. Arrange the papaya slices with the fish and return the platter to the warm oven while finishing the sauce.

Sprinkle the brown sugar into the skillet. Stir in the remaining 3 tablespoons lime juice and bring to a boil. Continue cooking, stirring constantly, until sauce thickens, approximately 1-1/2 to 2 minutes. Spoon the lime sauce over the fish and papaya slices and serve immediately.

Serves 4

Cajun Blackened Snapper and Pasta Salad

Dressing
    1/4 cup red wine vinegar
    2 large cloves garlic, pressed or minced
    1/4 teaspoon cayenne
    1 teaspoon honey
    1/4 teaspoon salt or to taste
    1/2 teaspoon dried thyme leaves
    1/2 teaspoon dried oregano leaves
    3/4 cup olive oil

Fish
    4 small red snapper fillets, 1/4 pound each
    4 tablespoons Blackened Seafood Seasoning
    1/4 cup melted butter
    2 tablespoons olive oil

Pasta
    12 ounces angel hair pasta
    1 large tomato
    2 hard boiled eggs
    1 lime cut into wedges

Place the vinegar, garlic, salt, cayenne, honey, thyme, and oregano into a blender or food processor. Process for a few seconds to blend and with motor still running, slowly drizzle in the oil. Chill until ready to use.

Heat a large cast-iron skillet for 10 minutes over high heat until VERY hot. (There is no such thing as too hot for this dish!) While skillet is heating, melt the butter in a separate pan. Dip the fish fillets generously in the butter and coat both sides with the blackened seafood seasoning. Carefully place the seasoned fillets in the hot skillet and quickly drizzle 1/2 tablespoon olive oil over each. The smoke and noise are all part of the act, so stand back. Let the fillets cook for 2 minutes, then turn and cook 2 minutes longer on the other side. Remove the fish and let cool.

Dice the tomato and the hard boiled eggs. Cook the pasta to desired doneness, rinse with cold water, and drain well. Toss with 3/4 cup of the salad dressing, the tomatoes, and eggs. Chill until ready to use.

Place a bed of pasta on four salad plates. Place a blackened fish fillet in the center of each. Drizzle the remaining dressing over the fish and pasta. Garnish the plates with lime wedges and serve at room temperature or chilled.

Serves 4

Note: If you are unable to find Blackened Seafood Seasoning in the fresh seafood section of your local market, it is very easy to prepare and keeps for several months. Combine the following: 3 tablespoons sweet paprika, 1 teaspoon dried thyme leaves, 1 teaspoon dried oregano leaves, 1 tablespoon onion powder, 1 tablespoon garlic powder, 1-1/2 tablespoons salt, 1 tablespoon cayenne, 2 tablespoons white pepper, and 2 tablespoons freshly ground black pepper. Store in an airtight jar in a cool, dark location.

Green Goddess Salad Dressing

1 clove garlic
3 tablespoons anchovies or anchovy paste
3 tablespoons chives or scallions, chopped
1 tablespoon lemon juice
3 tablespoons tarragon wine vinegar
1/2 cup sour cream
1 cup mayonnaise
1/3 cup chopped parsley
Salt and pepper to taste

Combine ingredients in order given. Chill. Serve on coarsely torn mixed greens.

Makes 2 cups.

Bleu Cheese/Buttermilk Dressing

1-1/2 cups sour cream
1 tablespoon Worcestershire sauce
1 tablespoon minced shallots
2/3 teaspoon garlic powder
1/2 teaspoon salt
1/2 teaspoon pepper
5 drops of Tabasco sauce
2 tablespoons lemon juice
3 cups mayonnaise
6 ounces bleu cheese
1/2 cup buttermilk

Blend sour cream, Worcestershire sauce, shallots, garlic powder, salt, pepper, Tabasco sauce, and lemon juice in a food processor for 2 minutes at low speed. Add mayonnaise; blend 1/2 minute at low speed, then blend 2 minutes at medium speed. Crumble bleu cheese by hand into very small pieces and add buttermilk. Blend at low speed no longer than 4 minutes. Chill 24 hours before using.

Makes 5 cups

Sour Cream Dressing

1 cup sour cream
2 tablespoons sugar
1 tablespoon vinegar
1/4 teaspoon salt
1/8 teaspoon pepper
3 green onions, sliced thin

Mix together thoroughly and refrigerate.

Makes 1-1/2 cups

Summer Solstice

Black Bean and Corn Salad   82
Black Beans with Tomatoes and Bleu Cheese   83
Caesar Potato Salad   93
Crab Fiesta Salad   90
Cucumber-Dill Relish   80
Fettucini with Yogurt and Basil   81
Lime Mayonnaise and Shrimp   80
Pasta and Vegetables   87
Pasta Pesto Marinara   85
Pasta Shells with Spicy Seafood Sauce   92
Pasta with Prosciutto and Peas   91
Pasta with Rainbow Bell Peppers   86
Penne with Cheese, Tomatoes, Olives, and Arugula   82
Ricotta Basil Olive Tart   84
Shrimp Linguine   88
South of the Border Spinach Salad   89
Tarragon Chicken and Pasta Salad   83
Tortellini Salad with Sun Dried Tomatoes   81

Lime Mayonnaise and Shrimp

2 cups mayonnaise
1/4 cup Dijon mustard
1/4 cup lime juice
2 tablespoons Worcestershire sauce
4 teaspoons Tabasco sauce
1 teaspoon grated lime peel
1/4 teaspoon cayenne
Salt and pepper
40 medium shrimp, cooked, peeled, and chilled (tails left on)
Lime wedges
Grated lime peel
Cayenne

Start two days before serving. Mix first 8 ingredients in small bowl. Cover and refrigerate for two days to blend flavors. Top with lime peel and cayenne. Surround with shrimp and lime wedges. Dip shrimp in sauce.

Cucumber-Dill Relish

4 cucumbers
1/3 cup chopped red onion
1/2 cup distilled white vinegar
4 teaspoons chopped fresh dill
2 teaspoons salt
1 teaspoon freshly ground pepper

Peel, seed, and coarsely grate cucumber. Squeeze dry by handfuls. Combine with remaining ingredients. Chill for at least 3 hours. Drain and serve.

Serves 6

Tortellini Salad with Sun Dried Tomatoes

    1 box tortellini filled with cheese
       (cooked according to package)
    3 cloves garlic
    1 cup sliced red onion
    1 small can sliced black olives
    1 cup toasted pine nuts
    1/2 cup fresh Parmesan
    1/3 cup olive oil
    1 package sun dried tomatoes, blanched and sliced

Cook and drain tortellini. Mix warm pasta with all the remaining ingredients. May be served warm or at room temperature.

Serves 4

Fettucini with Yogurt and Basil

    1 pound pasta
    1 cup yogurt
    2 cloves garlic, crushed
    1/2 cup fresh basil, chopped
    1/4 cup milk
    1 cup Parmesan, freshly grated

Cook fettucini until soft. Drain noodles. In pot add all other ingredients except cheese. Stir and then add cheese and fettucini. Add more yogurt or milk to taste if needed. Serve with topping of shredded basil.

Serves 4

Penne with Cheese, Tomatoes, Olives, and Arugula

1 pound fresh penne pasta
4-5 cloves garlic, minced
1/3 to 1/2 cup extra virgin olive oil
1 pound fresh arugula
5-6 Italian salad tomatoes, quartered
1/2 cup freshly grated Parmesan cheese
1/2 cup freshly grated Romano cheese
1/4 cup black Greek olives, pitted

Cook and drain pasta. Sauté garlic in oil until soft, approximately 5 minutes. Add tomatoes and arugula and sauté until arugula wilts and tomatoes are hot. Add 1/4 cup Parmesan and 1/4 cup Romano cheese and toss. Remove from heat and add olives. Serve topped with remaining cheese.

Serves 8

Black Bean and Corn Salad

1 16-ounce can black beans, drained
8 ounces frozen corn
4 cherry tomatoes, cut up
1/4 red pepper (or green), sliced
4 green onions, chopped
1/4 bunch cilantro leaves
1 clove garlic, minced
2 tablespoons vinegar
Pinch cayenne

Cook corn 2 minutes, drain, and put into medium-sized mixing bowl. Drain beans and add them and all remaining ingredients to bowl. Toss and serve. May be made and refrigerated a day ahead.

Serves 6

Black Beans with Tomatoes and Bleu Cheese

5 Italian salad tomatoes, diced
1 tablespoon finely minced shallots
1/2 cup bleu or Roquefort cheese, crumbled
1/2 pound black beans, rinsed and drained
2 tablespoons balsamic vinegar, or to taste
4 tablespoons extra virgin olive oil
2 tablespoons fresh parsley, finely minced
2 tablespoons fresh arugula, finely minced
Freshly ground black pepper, to taste

Combine all ingredients and allow flavors to blend for at least 30 minutes. Excellent with sour cream enchiladas, huevos rancheros, fish, and chicken.

Serves 6

Tarragon Chicken and Pasta Salad

1 cup mayonnaise
1 cup sour cream
1/4 cup Parmesan cheese, grated
1 tablespoon tarragon
1-1/2 pounds chicken, cooked and shredded
1-1/4 pounds pasta, cooked
1/3 bunch celery, sliced
1/3 bunch green onions, sliced
1/2 pound frozen peas
1/3 cup pistachio nuts

Mix together mayonnaise, sour cream, cheese, and tarragon. Add this to the remaining ingredients and mix in a bowl.

Serves 8-10

Ricotta Basil Olive Tart

Pastry
- 1 cup plus 3 tablespoons unbleached flour
- 1 teaspoon salt
- 10 tablespoons chilled unsalted butter
- 1/4 cup club soda, chilled

Place flour and salt in food processor. Add butter and pulse until crumbly. Add enough cold club soda to process into ball. Wrap in plastic wrap and refrigerate at least 30 minutes. Preheat oven to 400°. Press pastry into 10-inch tart pan. Prick all over with fork. Cover with wax paper and weight with beans. Bake for 20 minutes.

Filling
- 2 cups fresh basil, coarsely chopped
- 1 cup fresh Italian parsley, coarsely chopped
- 1/2 cup Ricotta cheese
- 1/2 cup Parmesan cheese, freshly grated
- 3 tablespoons olive oil
- 1 egg
- 1 egg yolk
- Salt and pepper, to taste
- 12 pitted black olives

While tart is baking, add everything except olives to food processor, process until mixed well. Transfer to bowl. Cut olives into small pieces and add to bowl. Correct seasoning. Remove tart shell from oven. Reduce heat to 350°. Remove beans and add Ricotta mixture. Return to oven for 30 minutes or until tart is set. Serve at room temperature.

Serves 6-8

Pasta Pesto Marinara

4 chopped tomatoes
2 chopped red onions
2 chopped celery stalks
1 chopped bell pepper (green and red)
1 tablespoon butter
1 tablespoon chopped garlic
Spices to taste (oregano, thyme, basil)
8 large shrimp or a bunch of small ones
1/4 cup wine
1 pound spinach fettucini
Pesto
3/4 cup pesto mixed with cream (1/4 cup)

Sauté tomatoes, onions, celery, and peppers in butter. Add garlic and spices. Stir mixture a bit then add shrimp and wine. Cook thoroughly. Cook fettucini and mix with pesto and cream. Spoon marinara on top of fettucine and pesto.

Serves 4

Pasta with Rainbow Bell Peppers

1/2 cup olive oil
2 large fillet of anchovies
3 cloves garlic
2 each yellow, red, and purple bell peppers
1 tablespoon dried oregano
1/2 cup black olives
1 tablespoon capers
4 to 5 large basil leaves, fresh
Salt and pepper, to taste
1 pound spaghetti

In a large frying pan, cut anchovies into small pieces and place in oil. Cook over medium heat. With a wooden spoon, stir anchovies until almost dissolved. Add thinly sliced garlic and let brown lightly. Wash peppers, eliminate top and inside and slice vertically (approximately 1-inch thick strips). Place peppers in oil and stir until slightly brown. Add oregano, olives (whole with pits), capers (hand squeezed dry), and basil, cut by hand in small pieces. Salt and pepper to taste. Cook spaghetti in salted water for 8 minutes. Drain. Add spaghetti to sauce, mix, stir constantly for 1 or 2 minutes. Serve at once. Can be served cold if prepared 4 or 5 hours in advance.

Serves 6

Pasta and Vegetables

- 1 **pound spaghetti**
- 1 **cup broccoli florets**
- 1 **cup 1-inch asparagus pieces**
- 1 **cup sugar snap peas**
- 1 **small zucchini or yellow summer squash, unpeeled, sliced in 1/2 lengthwise, then cut into 1-inch chunks**
- 1 **cup corn kernels**
- 1 **tablespoon garlic, finely minced**
- 1 **tablespoon olive oil**
- 1 **large tomato, diced**
- 1/2 **cup mushrooms, sliced**
- 1/2 **cup carrot, shredded**
- 1/4 **cup parsley, finely minced**
- 1/2 **teaspoon freshly ground black pepper**

Steam broccoli, asparagus, peas, zucchini, and corn for 5 minutes. Meanwhile, sauté garlic in oil for 1 minute, but DO NOT brown garlic. Add rest of ingredients and cook 4 minutes. Toss with reserved vegetables. Cook spaghetti or linguine al dente, drain, and keep warm.

Sauce
- 2 **teaspoon butter or margarine**
- 1 **tablespoon flour**
- 1 **cup skim or 1-percent milk**
- 1/2 **cup chicken stock**
- 1/2 **cup grated Parmesan**
- 1/4 **cup finely minced fresh basil or 1 teaspoon dried basil**

In small sauce pan melt butter, add flour, whisking roux over medium-low heat 1 minute. Gradually add milk and stock, stirring constantly until sauce slightly thickens. Stir in Parmesan and basil. Heat the sauce over medium-low flame, stirring until cheese melts. Pour sauce over vegetable mixture and toss.

Shrimp Linguine

1/2 pound linguine
10 large shrimp, shelled, deveined, and halved
1 tablespoon chopped fresh basil
1/2 cup olive oil
3 cloves garlic, minced
1 cup chopped zucchini
2 cups sliced mushrooms
2 cups tomatoes, peeled, seeded, and chopped
3/4 cup dry white wine
Juice of 1/2 lemon

Pour half of oil into skillet over medium heat. Sauté the garlic and basil for 3 minutes. Add the mushrooms and zucchini and sauté until tender crisp. Add wine and tomatoes and continue to cook. In another pan sauté shrimp in remaining oil until barely pink. Add lemon juice and cook until almost done. Stir in vegetables and cook until shrimp are done. Serve over hot linguine.

Serves 4

South of the Border Spinach Salad

1 large avocado, halved and peeled
1/3 cup sour cream
1/2 teaspoon lemon juice
1/4 teaspoon chili powder
1/4 cup milk
4 cups fresh spinach, torn
1 can garbanzo beans, chilled and drained
8 cherry tomatoes, halved
1/2 small cucumber, thinly sliced
1 cup sliced fresh mushrooms
1 small red onion, thinly sliced
1 can black olives, sliced
2 eggs, hard-cooked and chilled
1 teaspoon cilantro

For dressing, mash half of the avocado. Stir together mashed avocado, sour cream, lemon juice, and chili powder. Stir in milk. Cover and chill while preparing salad. For salad, combine spinach, garbanzo beans, tomatoes, cucumber, olives, mushrooms, onion, and cilantro. Add sliced egg and avocado. Top with dressing, toss to mix.

Serves 4

Crab Fiesta Salad

2 tablespoons salad oil
1 small onion, finely chopped
2 cloves garlic, minced or pressed
2 teaspoons paprika
1/2 teaspoon ground red pepper (cayenne)
1/2 teaspoon thyme
5 medium pear shaped (Roma) tomatoes
    (about 1 pound), chopped
1 pound cooked crab meat
3 tablespoons lemon juice
1/3 cup fresh cilantro
2 green onions, including tops, thinly sliced
Iceberg lettuce leaves, washed and crisped
Lemon wedges
Salt

Heat oil in a wide frying pan over medium heat. Add chopped onion and garlic. Cook, stirring often, until onion is tender (4-5 minutes). Stir in paprika, red pepper, thyme, and half the tomatoes. Cook uncovered stirring occasionally, until sauce is reduced to a thick pulp (about 5 minutes). Remove from heat and stir in crab and lemon juice. Let cool (at least 30 minutes). Stir in cilantro and about 1 cup of the remaining tomatoes; season to taste with salt. Line a platter with lettuce; spoon crab mixture on top. Garnish with remaining tomatoes and green onions. Serve with lemon wedges.

Serves 5-6

Pasta with Prosciutto and Peas

4 ounces Parmesan cheese, grated
1/3 cup basil leaves
1/3 cup parsley leaves
2 tablespoons sage leaves
1 large garlic clove, peeled
3 medium shallots, peeled
2 tablespoons olive oil
2 tablespoons unsalted butter
6 ounces prosciutto, cut into 1/4-inch dice
3/4 cup heavy cream
1/2 teaspoon salt
1/4 teaspoon crushed red pepper flakes
1/4 teaspoon freshly ground black pepper
12 ounces pastina or other small pasta
1 package frozen peas

Grate Parmesan cheese and reserve. Chop the basil, parsley, and sage and put aside. Mince garlic and shallots and cook in the oil and butter in a large skillet over medium-high heat until softened, about 3 minutes. Add the prosciutto and cook for 3 minutes. Add the herbs, cream, salt, crushed red pepper, and black pepper and cook until the sauce is thickened, about 5 minutes. Meanwhile, cook the pasta in boiling salted water until al dente, about 4 minutes, adding the peas in the last 30 seconds. Drain and return to the pan. Stir in the prosciutto mixture and Parmesan.

Serves 8

Pasta Shells with
Spicy Seafood Sauce

1/2 cup basil leaves
3 garlic cloves
1 small carrot
1 celery rib
1 onion
1 35-ounce can plum tomatoes, reserve 1/2 cup juice
3 tablespoons olive oil
1 teaspoon crushed red pepper flakes
1 pound shrimp, medium sized
1 pound pasta shells
1/4 teaspoon saffron threads, crumbled
1/2 teaspoon grated lemon zest
1/2 teaspoon grated orange zest

Chop basil and put aside. Mince garlic and add to chopped carrot, celery and onion. Cook vegetable mixture in 2 tablespoons olive oil in a skillet until softened. Add tomatoes, reserved juice, and peppers. Simmer for 7 minutes. Cook the shelled and halved-lengthwise shrimp in 1 tablespoon oil in a skillet about 2 minutes. Set aside. Cook pasta shells in salted water until soft (10 minutes). Drain, reserving 1 tablespoon water. Dissolve saffron in reserved water and add to the tomato mixture with the basil and zests. Toss pasta shells with the sauce and the shrimp.

Serves 6

Caesar Potato Salad

8   cups small red potatoes, skinned and diced
1   egg
2   anchovies, or 2 teaspoons anchovy paste
2   garlic cloves, minced
1/4   cup lemon juice
1/2   cup Parmesan cheese, grated
1/2   cup olive oil
Salt and pepper
1/3   cup scallions, sliced
1/4   cup fresh parsley, minced

Boil the potatoes until just tender, about 10 minutes. Drain and place in a large bowl to cool slightly. In a food processor or blender, combine the egg, anchovies, garlic, lemon juice, and cheese. Process until smooth. With the processor running, slowly pour in the oil in a thin stream. The dressing will thicken slightly. Season to taste with salt and pepper. Pour the dressing over the potatoes, and add the scallions and parsley and toss. Chill the salad 2 hours.

Serves 6-8

Sides

Pine Nut and Orange Wild Rice

5 cups water
1 cup wild rice
1 cup brown rice
1 cup dried currants
1/2 cup pine nuts, toasted
4 tablespoons cilantro, chopped
2 tablespoons grated orange zest
1/4 cup olive oil
2 tablespoons orange juice, freshly squeezed
Freshly ground black pepper to taste
Parmesan cheese, freshly grated

Pour 3 cups of water in a saucepan. Bring to a boil and add wild rice. Stir, reduce heat, cover, and simmer for 25 minutes. Drain, if necessary, and place in a large bowl. Pour the remaining 2 cups of water in a separate saucepan. Bring to a boil and add the brown rice. Stir, reduce heat, cover the pan, and simmer for 15 minutes. Place in the bowl with the wild rice.

Gently toss remaining ingredients, except the grated cheese, with the two rices. (Rice can be prepared 3 hours ahead to this point. Cover but do not refrigerate.) An hour before serving, preheat oven to 350°.

Place rice in an ovenproof casserole and cover with aluminum foil. Before serving, heat through for 20 minutes. After heating, sprinkle with freshly grated Parmesan cheese.

Serves 6-8

Asparagus with Orange Butter Sauce

1/2 cup butter
1/3 cup minced shallots
1-1/4 teaspoons Dijon mustard
1-1/3 cups orange juice
2 pounds asparagus
Salt
6 orange wedges

In a large frying pan, melt 1 tablespoon butter over medium heat. Add shallots and stir until soft. Add mustard and orange juice. Bring to a boil over high heat; boil, uncovered, until reduced to 2/3 cup, about 10 minutes. Set aside.

Discard tough ends of asparagus. In a large frying pan, bring about 1 inch of water to a boil over high heat. Add asparagus, reduce heat and simmer, uncovered until barely tender when pierced, 3-5 minutes.

Reheat orange juice mixture to boiling, then reduce heat to low. Add remaining 7 tablespoons of butter a chunk at a time. Season with salt to taste.

Garnish asparagus with orange halves and pass the sauce.

Serves 6

Peas with Rosemary and Pine Nuts

1/2 cup chicken stock
2 green onions, chopped into 1/2 inch pieces
1/2 teaspoon sugar
2 10-ounce packages frozen petite peas, thawed

Bring first three ingredients to simmer. Add peas and cook 3 minutes. Drain.

3 tablespoons butter
1/2 cup pine nuts
1 tablespoon fresh rosemary, minced,
   or 1 teaspoon dried and crumbled
Salt and pepper

Melt butter in skillet and add pine nuts. Stir until golden, then mix in rosemary. Cook 1 minute. Add peas and green onions. Cook until hot.

Serves 8-10

Artichokes Aurora

2 tablespoons olive oil
1/2 pound spinach, washed and trimmed
1/4 pound mushrooms, sliced
1/4 cup onion, chopped
1 small clove garlic, minced
1/4 cup Parmesan cheese, grated
1/2 teaspoon thyme
1/4 teaspoon salt
Pepper to taste
1/3 cup slivered almonds
1 lemon or lime, sliced
2 small artichokes

Boil artichokes in lots of water for 30-40 minutes. Drain and cool enough to handle.

Heat oil in skillet, sauté spinach several minutes. Add mushrooms, onion, and garlic. Cook over high heat, stirring often, until no liquid appears in bottom of skillet. Remove from heat. Add Parmesan cheese, thyme, salt, and pepper. Mix well. Stir in almonds.

Cut tops off artichokes. Cut tips off outer leaves. Peel off bottom leaves. Open artichoke leaves slightly and remove center leaves and spiky leaves next to heart. Place lemon/lime slices in bottom of cavity of each artichoke. Fill cavity with spinach mixture. Place artichokes in deep baking dish. Pour 2 cups of water around them. Cover and bake in 375° oven for 30-40 minutes. Serve hot with vinaigrette.

Serves 2

Cold Asparagus
with Mustard-Tarragon Vinaigrette

2 pounds fresh asparagus
1/4 cup Dijon mustard
3 tablespoons boiling water
1/3-1/2 cup olive oil
2 tablespoons vinegar
Salt and pepper
1 tablespoon fresh tarragon, or 1 teaspoon dried tarragon

Parboil asparagus until just tender. Drain and refresh with cold water.

Prepare dressing by slowly beating the boiling water into mustard with wire whisk. Slowly beat in olive oil until you have a thick creamy sauce. Add vinegar a little at a time until pleasantly tart. Season with salt, pepper, and tarragon.

Serves 8

Beets in Orange Sauce

6 large beets, sliced
3 tablespoons brown sugar
1/4 stick of butter, cut into bits
1-1/2 cups fresh orange juice
1/2 teaspoon salt

Layer beets in glass pan, cover with the remaining ingredients. Bake covered at 350° for 45 to 60 minutes.

Serves 4-6

Broccoli and Grapefruit Bake

1 **egg white**
1/4 **cup mayonnaise or salad dressing**
3 **tablespoons Parmesan cheese, grated**
2 **tablespoons parsley, chopped**
1 **tablespoon grapefruit peel, freshly grated**
2 **10-ounce packages frozen broccoli, cooked and drained**
1 **grapefruit, peeled, sectioned**
2 **tablespoons butter or margarine, melted**

In small bowl, beat egg white until soft peaks form. Fold in mayonnaise. Stir in cheese, parsley, and grapefruit peel. Arrange cooked broccoli and grapefruit sections in ovenproof serving dish. Pour melted butter over broccoli and grapefruit; top with egg white mixture. Bake at 450° for 5 minutes of until puffy and lightly brown. Surprisingly delicious and great served with fish.

Serves 4-6

Puffy Broccoli Cheese Bake

1 **egg white**
1/4 **cup mayonnaise**
3 **tablespoons Parmesan cheese, grated**
2 **tablespoons parsley, chopped**
Grated peel of 1/2 fresh lemon
2 **pounds fresh, or 2, 10-ounce packages frozen, broccoli, cooked and drained**
2 **tablespoon butter or margarine, melted**

In small bowl, beat egg white until soft peaks form. Fold in mayonnaise. Stir in cheese, parsley, and lemon peel. Arrange cooked broccoli in oven proof serving dish. Pour melted butter over broccoli; top with egg white mixture. Bake at 450° for 5 minutes or until puffy and lightly brown.

Serves 4-6

Brussels Sprouts in Dill Walnut Sauce

1-1/2 pounds fresh Brussels sprouts
3/4 cup scallions
3 tablespoons fresh parsley
2 tablespoons fresh dill
3 tablespoons lemon juice
3 ounces walnuts
4 tablespoons butter
Salt and pepper to taste

Prepare Brussels sprouts and steam until tender. Drain and transfer to serving bowl. In food processor, combine scallions, parsley, dill, lemon juice, walnuts, and butter. Blend the mixture until smooth. Pour dressing over Brussels sprouts. Toss.

Serves 6

Glazed Carrots and Grapes

1 pound carrots
1 tablespoon brown sugar
1 teaspoon salt
3 tablespoons butter
1 tablespoon flour
4 tablespoons brown sugar
1/4 cup orange juice
2 tablespoons Vodka
1 cup red seedless grapes

Cut carrots in 1-inch diagonal slices. Cook covered in water sweetened with brown sugar and salt. Cook until barely tender, about 20 minutes.

Melt butter in saucepan, add flour and blend. Add brown sugar. Stir in orange juice. Add grapes and heat through. Add Vodka, heat through. Stir on cooked carrots until coated with glaze.

Serves 8

Carrot Soufflé

1 pound carrots, peeled and cut into 1-inch chunks
4 large eggs
3/4 cup flour
1/8 teaspoon salt
1 teaspoon baking powder
1/2 cup sugar
1 tablespoon butter, softened
2 teaspoons vanilla
1 teaspoon nutmeg
2-1/2 tablespoons orange rind, grated

Cook carrots until tender. Purée in food processor and let cool to room temperature. Preheat oven to 350°. Butter a 1-quart soufflé dish. Beat eggs one at a time with a mixer, beating for 2 minutes after the addition of each egg. Sift together flour, salt, and baking powder. Add flour mixture to carrots and process until blended. Add eggs, sugar, butter, vanilla, and nutmeg. Process until well combined. Pour into soufflé dish and sprinkle with orange rind. Bake 40 minutes, or until puffed and firm.

Serves 4 - 6

Carrots with Thyme

1 pound carrots
1/2 stick butter
1/4 cup water
1/2 teaspoon thyme
Grated zest of one lemon
1 teaspoon sugar
Salt and pepper
Chopped fresh parsley

Peel carrots and julienne. Melt butter in skillet, add water, carrots, thyme, lemon zest, sugar, salt, and pepper. Cook slowly, partially covered until carrots are tender, approximately 20-25 minutes. Sprinkle with parsley.

Serves 8

Celery Amandine

4 cups celery, sliced diagonally
1/2 cup almonds, slivered
1/4 cup chicken stock
1 teaspoon parsley, minced
2 tablespoons butter
1/2 teaspoon sugar
Dash of garlic powder
Salt to taste

In sauce pan, melt butter. Add celery, chicken stock, and garlic powder. Cover and cook over low heat for about 10 minutes or until tender crisp, stirring occasionally. Add salt, sugar, and almonds. Cook 2-3 minutes longer. Sprinkle with parsley and serve.

Serves 4-6

Cauliflower with Goat Cheese

4 tablespoons unsalted butter
1-1/4 cups heavy cream
1/2 teaspoons salt
1/4 teaspoons white pepper, freshly ground
1 large head of cauliflower (about 1-1/2 pounds),
    separated into florets
1/4 pound of lightly smoked ham,
    cut into 1/4 inch diced pieces
1/4 cup coarsely crumbled mild goat cheese,
    such as Montrachet or a fresh American goat cheese
    (about 2 ounces)
4 ounces Fontina cheese, grated

In a large heavy saucepan, melt 2 tablespoons of the butter over moderate heat. Add the cream and boil until reduced to 3/4 cup, about 10 minutes. Season with salt and white pepper. Remove from heat.

Meanwhile, steam the cauliflower for 5-8 minutes, or until tender. Remove to a colander and set aside.

In a small skillet, melt 1 tablespoon of the butter. Add the ham and sauté over moderate heat until lightly browned, about 2 minutes.

Arrange the cauliflower in a buttered 6-cup gratin dish. Sprinkle the ham over the cauliflower. Spoon cream over the cauliflower and sprinkle with the Fontina and bits of goat cheese. Dot with the remaining 1 tablespoon butter. (The recipe can be set aside for a few hours before baking.)

Bake at 350° for 15 minutes. Increase to 450° and bake for 10 minutes longer. Serve hot.

Serves 4-6

Dolmas

1/2 cup oil
3 large onions, finely chopped
1 cup long grain rice
1 cup parsley, minced
1/4 cup pine nuts, toasted
Salt and pepper to taste
18 canned grape leaves, washed and drained
2-3 tablespoons fresh lemon juice
2 tablespoons olive oil

Heat oil in skillet and sauté onions until transparent. Add rice and cook 10 minutes. Add parsley, nuts, salt, and pepper. Simmer for 5 minutes or until liquid is absorbed. Cool slightly before stuffing leaves. In the center of each leaf (shiny side down) place 1 teaspoon of filling. Fold sides over and, starting at stem end, roll up. Place rolls in heavy shallow pan with seam side down. Sprinkle with lemon juice and olive oil. Cover up to height of rolls with hot water and simmer on low flame for about 35 minutes. Cool dolmas, brush with oil and serve with lemon slices.

Serves 8-10

Eggplant with Tomatoes

2/3 cup extra virgin olive oil
4 cloves garlic, minced
2-1/2 pounds onions, halved, thinly sliced
1-1/2 pounds Japanese eggplant, skin on,
      cut into 1-inch cubes
1 pound zucchini, skin on, cut into 1/2-inch to 1-inch cubes
8 medium tomatoes, peeled, seeded, chopped
1-1/2 pounds red or green bell peppers, roasted, peeled,
      cut into strips
Salt and pepper to taste

Heat oil in a Dutch oven and add garlic, onions, eggplant, and zucchini. Stir well so that all vegetables are coated with oil. Cover the pan and cook 10 minutes on low heat. Uncover and turn heat up slightly, cooking until the liquid has evaporated. Stir occasionally.

Add the tomatoes and peppers, reduce heat, and simmer uncovered until the liquid has again evaporated and the vegetables are very soft. Season to taste.

Makes 6-8 cups

Braised Endive and Celery

6 whole endive
2 bunches celery hearts
3 tablespoons butter
1 bay leaf
1/4 teaspoons thyme
Juice of 1/2 lemon
1 cup chicken stock
Salt and pepper to taste

Cut each endive in half lengthwise. Trim tops from celery hearts and cut each one in half lengthwise. On top of stove, heat butter in bottom of casserole, add vegetables, seasonings, lemon juice and stock. Bring to a simmer, cover and simmer for 30 minutes or until tender. Drain and place on serving platter. Sprinkle with paprika for color.

Serves 6

"Haricot verts" with Tomatoes and Garlic

1 pound young "haricot verts" (green beans)
2 tomatoes, peeled, seeded and chopped
1 garlic clove, finely minced
1/4 cup parsley, minced
3 tablespoons butter
1 tablespoon olive oil

Steam or parboil beans for 3-4 minutes, drain and refresh with cold water. In skillet, heat butter and oil. Add tomatoes, garlic, and parsley; and cook until tomatoes cook down to a purée. Add beans, toss well and season with salt and pepper. Serve with fresh minced parsley.

Serves 6-8

Green Beans in Lemon Cream

1-1/2 pounds fresh green beans
4 tablespoons butter
3/4 cup heavy cream
1 egg
Salt to taste
White pepper to taste
2 tablespoons Parmesan cheese, grated
1/4 teaspoon nutmeg
Juice of 1 lemon

Clean, prepare and steam beans. Drain thoroughly. Return to saucepan. Add butter and 2 tablespoons cream. Cook over low heat for 2 minutes. Break egg in small bowl, add salt, pepper, remaining cream, Parmesan, nutmeg, and lemon juice. Stir until well mixed. Pour over beans and cook until sauce thickens and beans are well coated.

Serves 6-8

Baked Leeks

8 medium to large leeks
1/4 cup butter
1 cup heavy cream
Nutmeg to taste
Salt and white pepper to taste
Parmesan cheese, grated

Sauté leeks in butter until just wilted. Add nutmeg, salt, white pepper, and cream. Cook for 1 minute. With a slotted spoon, remove leeks from pan and place in buttered gratin dish. Cook cream over high heat until reduced slightly. Pour cream over leeks and sprinkle with cheese. Place gratin dish into another baking pan which has a small amount of water in it and bake at 350° for 30-35 minutes.

Serves 6-8

Baked Onions

6 large round unpeeled onions (Vidalia, Maui, or white)
Olive oil
Salt and pepper
Butter

Rub each onion with olive oil and sprinkle with salt and pepper. Wrap each onion in double thickness of foil and place on barbecue grill. Turn from time to time. Cook about 30-40 minutes. Remove from foil and season with butter, salt, and pepper.

Serves 6

Sautéed Apples and Onions

3-4 tart apples, peeled, cored, and sliced
1 medium onion, sliced
4 tablespoons butter
1/8 teaspoon sugar
1/8 teaspoon thyme
Salt and pepper
Lemon juice

In a large skillet, heat butter until foamy. Add onion and sauté. Add apples, sugar, thyme, salt, and pepper. Toss continually until apples are tender and golden. Sprinkle with lemon juice.

Serves 4-6

Peas with Prosciutto

  2 tablespoons butter
  4 tablespoons onion, finely chopped
  2 slices Prosciutto, cut in strips
  1 clove garlic
  1/4 cup white wine
  2 10-ounce packages frozen peas
  Salt and pepper

Melt butter in skillet, add onion and Prosciutto, and cook until onions are tender. Add garlic and wine. Add peas and simmer until tender. Season with salt and pepper to taste.

Serves 6

Sherried Sweet Potatoes

  8 small to medium-sized sweet potatoes
  1 cup brown sugar
  2 tablespoons cornstarch
  1/2 teaspoon salt
  1/2 tablespoon orange peel, grated
  2 cups orange juice
  6 tablespoons butter
  1/2 cup dry sherry
  1/4 cup chopped walnuts

Cook potatoes in boiling water until tender. Drain. Peel and cut lengthwise into 1/2-inch thick slices. Arrange in 9 x 13-inch baking dish. Sprinkle with salt. In sauce pan, blend orange peel, orange juice, and raisins. Cook and stir over medium heat until thickened, plus 1 minute more. Add butter, sherry, and walnuts. Pour over potatoes. Bake at 325° for 30 minutes, basting frequently.

Serves 8

Bleu Cheese Bacon Potatoes

4 medium potatoes
1/2 cup sour cream
1 ounce bleu cheese, crumbled
1/4 cup milk
4 tablespoons butter
3/4 teaspoon salt
Pepper to taste
4-6 slices of crisp bacon, crumbled

Wash potatoes and dry. Rub potatoes with extra butter and bake in 400° oven for 1 hour or until done. Remove from oven. Cut a lengthwise slice from each potato. Scoop out inside of each potato. Mash potatoes. Add sour cream, bleu cheese, milk, butter, salt, and pepper. Mix until smooth. Beat with electric mixer until fluffy. Spoon mixture lightly into potato shells. Place on baking sheet and return to hot oven for 15 minutes. Sprinkle with bacon and serve.

Serves 4

Potatoes Boulangerie

5-6 medium potatoes, thinly sliced
1 onion, thinly sliced
1 tablespoon parsley, chopped
3 tablespoons butter
2 cups beef bouillon

Layer one half of the potatoes, onions, and parsley in a 2-quart casserole. Repeat, top with butter. Pour bouillon over all. Bake in a 375° oven 2 hours until well done and browned.

Serves 6

Brazilian Rice

3 cups cooked rice
2 bunches spinach, cooked, drained, and chopped
16 ounces brick cheese, grated
1 small onion, minced, sautéed in 2 tablespoons butter
1/2 teaspoon marjoram
1/2 teaspoon thyme
1/2 teaspoon rosemary
1 tablespoon Worcestershire sauce
1 cup milk (whole)
4 eggs, lightly beaten

Combine rice, spinach, and cheese. Add onion and herbs. Stir in remaining ingredients. Mix well. Pour into 9 x 13-inch baking dish. Bake at 350° for 30-40 minutes.

Serves 6-8

Crunchy Wild Rice

4 strips bacon, cooked and crumbled
1/2 cup onion, chopped
1 clove garlic, minced
1 stalk celery, diced
1/2 cup chopped water chestnuts
1/4 cup sherry
1 6-ounce package long grain and wild rice, cooked

Fry bacon and set aside. Pour off all but 2 tablespoons grease. Sauté onion, garlic, and celery until tender. Stir in water chestnuts, sherry, cooked rice and crumbled bacon.

Serves 4

Two-Grain Salad
with Green Beans and Pine Nuts

1 cup barley (not quick-cooking)
1 cup bulgur
1/4 cup fresh lemon juice
1 teaspoon Dijon mustard
3/4 cup olive oil
1 pound green beans, trimmed
1/2 cup pine nuts, toasted lightly

In a saucepan, combine the barley with 6 cups boiling water and simmer for 40 minutes. Drain the barley in a colander, rinse it, and drain it well. In a bowl combine the bulgur with 1-1/2 cups boiling salted water and let the mixture stand, fluffing it with a fork occasionally, for 20-30 minutes, or until all the water is absorbed. Add the barley and toss the mixture until it is combined well.

In a small bowl, whisk together the lemon juice, mustard, and salt and pepper to taste; add the oil in a stream, whisking until it is emulsified. Add the dressing to the grain mixture and toss the mixture until it is combined well. (The mixture may be prepared up to this point one day in advance and kept covered and chilled.)

In a kettle of boiling salted water, cook the green beans for 4-5 minutes, or until they are just tender. Slice the beans thin crosswise, add them to the grain mixture with the pine nuts and salt and pepper to taste, and toss the salad until it is combined well.

Serves 6 to 8

Spinach Ramekin

Filling
 1 10-ounce package frozen spinach
 1 tablespoon onion, finely chopped
Ramekin mixture
 1/2 cup flour
 2 cups cold milk
 3-1/2 tablespoons butter
 1/2 teaspoon salt
 Dash white pepper
 4 eggs
 1-1/3 cups grated Swiss cheese

Place flour in sauce pan and gradually beat in milk with wire whisk. Stir slowly over moderately high heat until mixture comes to a boil and thickens. Remove from heat. Beat in butter, seasonings, and one by one the eggs. Beat in 1 cup of cheese. Turn one-half the mixture into buttered dish, spread spinach mixture on top and cover with rest of cheese mixture. Sprinkle on remaining cheese. Bake for 25 minutes at 400°.

Serves 8

Creamed Squash au Gratin

1 cup water
2 pounds yellow squash, sliced
1 teaspoon salt
1/8 teaspoon sugar
1/4 cup butter, softened
1-1/4 cups sharp Cheddar, cubed
1 cup sour cream or yogurt
1/2 cup onion, chopped fine
1/3 cup Parmesan cheese, grated
1/4 cup dry white wine
Salt and pepper to taste
1 cup bread crumbs
3 tablespoons butter, melted

Bring water to a boil in saucepan. Add squash, salt, and sugar, and cook, covered, over moderate heat until squash is tender (about 20 minutes). Drain. Add butter and mash (do not use food processor) until mixture is well blended. Stir in Cheddar cheese, sour cream or yogurt, onion, Parmesan cheese, white wine, salt, and pepper to taste. Pour into 11-inch au gratin dish and top with bread crumbs, which have been combined with the melted butter. Bake in a preheated moderate oven (350°) for 20-30 minutes, or until bubbling and golden on top.

Serves 6

Herbed Tomatoes

12 small tomatoes, peeled (not cherry tomatoes)
1 teaspoon salt
1/4 teaspoon pepper
Several fresh thyme or marjoram leaves
1/4 cup parsley, chopped
1/4 cup chives, chopped
2/3 cup salad oil
1/4 cup tarragon vinegar

Mix all ingredients except tomatoes. Add tomatoes and marinate for at least 2 hours or overnight.

Hint: Blanch tomatoes in boiling water for a few seconds to ease peeling.

Serves 12

Tomatoes Stuffed with Duchesse Potatoes

6 medium potatoes
Boiling water
1 teaspoon salt
1/8 teaspoon white pepper
1/4 teaspoon nutmeg
2 whole eggs
2 egg yolks
1/4 green onion, chopped
1/4 cup Parmesan cheese
6 medium tomatoes, washed and dried

Peel potatoes, cut in cubes, boil in water with salt until soft. Drain. Beat with an electric mixer on low until potatoes are mashed. Add pepper, onions, and nutmeg. Beat all eggs together until foamy and add to potatoes. Whip mixture until fluffy.

Stuffed tomatoes: Cut small slice off bottoms of tomatoes to rest on. Cut off top third of tomato with zig zag cut. Scoop out center. Sprinkle lightly with salt and pepper. Invert on tray to drain well. Fill cookie press with Duchesse potatoes. Pipe into tomatoes, heaping over top. Sprinkle with Parmesan cheese. Brush with melted butter. Brown in preheated oven (450°) for 10 minutes.

Serves 6

Zucchini Fans with Herb Butter

1 tablespoon bread crumbs
2 tablespoons Parmesan cheese
1/4 cup unsalted butter, softened
1/2 teaspoon dried tarragon, crumbled
2 tablespoons fresh parsley, minced
4 6-inch zucchini
Salt and pepper to taste

In a small bowl toss bread crumbs and Parmesan. In second bowl, cream butter, tarragon, parsley, salt, and pepper. Keeping the stem attached, cut each zucchini lengthwise into four slices. Spread some of the herb butter carefully between the layers and press slices lightly together. Separate the slices slightly to form fan. Bake fans with 1/4 cup water in buttered baking pan in a preheated 400° oven for 20 minutes or until tender. Sprinkle with crumb mixture and broil 4 inches from heat for 2 minutes.

Serves 4

Curried Fruit

1 pound can each: pears, apricots, peaches, pineapple
  chunks, and seedless bing cherries
1 cup brown sugar
2 teaspoons curry powder
3/4 stick butter
1/2 teaspoon ground ginger or nutmeg
1/2 cup sherry

Drain fruit and cut into large pieces. Grease a 3-quart baking dish
with extra butter. In a small sauce pan, melt and cook together for
several minutes the sugar, curry powder, butter, and ginger. Put half
of mixed fruit in bottom of baking dish and pour half of the sauce
over. Repeat with remaining fruit and sauce. Pour sherry over all.
Cook in 350° oven for 1 hour. Serve hot in bowls or ramekins.

Serves 10-12

Papaya Walter

3 papayas, cut in half and seeded
1-1/2 cups cottage cheese
1-1/2 cups cream cheese
1 teaspoon curry powder
2 tablespoons chopped mango chutney
2 tablespoons golden raisins
1/2 cup water chestnuts, very thinly sliced
1/4 cup melted butter
Cinnamon to taste

Mix and blend cheeses, curry and chutney. When well blended and
smooth, add raisins and chestnuts. Fill papaya with cheese mixture.
Sprinkle top with cinnamon and melted butter. Bake for
approximately 15 minutes in 450° oven.

Serves 6

Apples and Yams

  2 large yams
  2 tablespoons butter
  Salt and pepper to taste
  Grated lemon peel of 1/2 lemon
  8 large apples
  1/4 teaspoon cinnamon
Syrup
  1 cup sugar
  1/2 cup water
  1-1/2 teaspoons grated orange peel, grated
  8 teaspoons butter

Bake yams in 400° oven for 1-1/2 hours or until tender. Cut yams and scoop out pulp. Mash or purée yams and add butter, salt, pepper, lemon peel. Hollow out apples, leaving bottoms intact. Slice off top of apple. Sprinkle cavity with cinnamon and fill apples with yam mixture.

In a saucepan combine sugar, water, and orange peel; bringing to a boil over medium heat. Put stuffed apples in oven proof dish. Pour in syrup, top each apple with 1 teaspoon butter. Bake 350°, basting every 10 minutes for 45 minutes to 1 hour.

Serves 8

Fiesta

Avocado Salsa

6 medium tomatoes, diced
3 or 4 serrano chiles with seeds, minced
1 medium onion, finely diced
3 tablespoons cilantro, chopped
2 tablespoons lime juice
1 teaspoon salt
1 medium avocado, peeled, pitted, and diced

Combine all ingredients and let sit at least 1/2 hour at room temperature to blend flavors. Drain off excess liquid before serving with chips.

Yield 5 cups

Salsa Colorado #1

Red sauce made from dried chiles

16 dried California chiles (chili ancho)
1 clove garlic
1 tablespoon lard
1 teaspoon salt
1 teaspoon sugar
1/2 teaspoon cinnamon
1/2 teaspoon cumin, ground
2 cups tomato sauce
2 cups water

Remove stems and veins from chiles. Cover with hot water and boil 10 minutes. Soak at least 1/2 hour. Drain. Put garlic and small amount of chiles in blender and blend well. Add remaining chiles and part of water and blend until very smooth. Melt lard. Add purée and cook about 5 minutes, stirring. Add tomato sauce slowly, simmer a few minutes. Add salt, sugar, cinnamon, ground cumin, and water. Cook 20 minutes.

Yield 4 cups

Salsa Colorado #2
Red sauce made from chili powder

2 tablespoons lard
4 tablespoons Gebhardts chili powder
1-1/2 cups tomato sauce
2-1/2 cups water
1 teaspoon sugar
1/2 teaspoon cinnamon
1 teaspoon salt

Melt lard, add chili powder and cook over low heat, stirring, 3-4 minutes. Add tomato slowly and simmer 10 minutes. Add water and spices. Add salt to taste. Cook 20 minutes.

Yield 4 cups

Peach Salsa

2 cups peeled, diced ripe peaches (2 medium)
1/2 cup red onion, diced
1/2 cup fresh sweet red pepper, diced
1/2 to 3/4 teaspoon jalapeño or serrano chili, finely minced
2 teaspoons olive oil
2 tablespoons fresh lime juice
1/4 cup fresh mint, finely chopped
2 teaspoons ginger, freshly grated

Combine all ingredients and serve. Better if made 1/2 hour ahead to blend flavors. Good with grilled or roast chicken, beef, or lamb.

Yield 3 cups

Pineapple Salsa

1 small fresh pineapple, cut into small cubes
1 small red onion, diced
1 medium sweet red pepper, cored, seeded and diced
1 medium sweet yellow or purple sweet pepper,
   cored, seeded and diced
1/2 to 3/4 teaspoons fresh jalapeño or serrano chili,
   finely minced
1 teaspoon ground cumin
1 teaspoon ground coriander
1 teaspoon fresh lime juice

Combine all ingredients and let flavors blend for a least 30 minutes. Good with swordfish, tuna, shrimp, or other fish.

Yield 4-5 cups

Salsa Para Pescados

2-1/2 tablespoons onion, chopped
1 clove garlic
1/3 lemon, sliced thin
2/3 tablespoon celery leaves, chopped
2/3 tablespoon parsley, chopped
2/3 tablespoon lemon juice
1-1/3 teaspoons honey
2/3 teaspoon olive oil
1-1/3 teaspoons whole wheat flour
1/3 teaspoon chili powder
2/3 cup tomato purée
1 hard boiled egg, chopped

Cook onion in oil until tender, add whole wheat flour, and allow to brown. Add remaining ingredients except egg. Simmer about 10 minutes. Add egg and serve over fish.

Yield 1 cup

Sizzle Salsa

5 tomatoes, finely chopped
1 onion, coarsely chopped
1 yellow chili, minced
1 jalapeño, minced
Juice of 1 lemon
1 small garlic, minced

Combine all ingredients and refrigerate until ready to use.

Yield 1 cup

Salsa Verde Green Sauce

2 pounds tomatillos (4 cans tomatillos enteros, 12-ounce size)
3 small chiles, jalapeños or serranos, stems removed
1 clove garlic
1 tablespoon lard
1 teaspoon salt, or to taste
1 cup water
1 small ball "masa" (tortilla dough) optional
1 sprig cilantro, chopped fine, optional

Remove husks from tomatillos and boil 15 minutes. If using canned tomatillos, omit this step. Drain tomatillos and blend with garlic and chiles. Blend thoroughly. Heat lard in deep saucepan. Add puréed tomatillos. Cook, stirring, 5 minutes. Add water, salt, and ball of masa. Simmer 10 minutes. Stir in cilantro chopped fine.

Yield 5 cups

Marinated Chiles

21 ounces green whole chiles
1 cup sugar
1 cup white vinegar
1 large clove of garlic, crushed
1 tablespoon dill weed (dried)
1/2 teaspoon salt
Slices of Monterey Jack cheese
Crackers or chips

Rinse and seed chiles. Cut the chiles into square size to fit cracker or chip. Combine the sugar, vinegar, garlic, dill weed, and salt. Marinate chiles in this mixture. The longer they marinate, the better, and they last several weeks if kept in refrigerator. Place a slice of Monterey Jack cheese and then a chili on cracker or chip and serve.

Roasted Pepper Spread

1 7-ounce jar roasted red peppers, drained
2 jalapeño chiles, seeded
4 large green olives, pitted
1 tablespoon fresh parsley
2 teaspoons olive oil
1-1/2 teaspoons fresh lemon juice
Salt and pepper
French bread or sesame crackers

In a food processor, finely chop the peppers, olives, and parsley. Add the olive oil and lemon juice and process just until mixed. Add salt and pepper to taste. Spread on French bread slices or sesame crackers.

Yields 1 cup

Shrimp Con Quesa Dip

1/2 cup onion, finely chopped
2 tomatoes, medium
4 ounce can green peppers, drained
1 cup shredded American cheese
1 cup shredded Monterey Jack cheese
1 teaspoon cornstarch
1/4 teaspoon chili powder
1/2 pound cooked shrimp

In saucepan, sauté onion in margarine until tender. Stir in tomatoes and peppers. Simmer, uncovered, 10 minutes. Toss cheeses with cornstarch and chili powder. Gradually add to saucepan, stirring until melted. Stir in cocktail shrimp. Serve warm with chips.

Yield 3 cups

Spicy Snapper Soup

1 medium onion, finely chopped
2 cloves garlic, minced or pressed
1/2 teaspoon dry oregano leaves
1/4 teaspoon cumin seeds, coarsely crushed
1 bay leaf
1 or 2 jalapeño chiles, seeded and chopped
1 can chicken broth
2-1/4 cups tomato juice
1 orange
1/2 pound snapper fillets
1/4 cup fresh cilantro
1 tablespoon olive oil
Salt
Lime wedges

Heat oil in a 3-quart pan over medium heat. Add onion, garlic, oregano, and cumin seeds; cook, stirring often, until onion is soft (about 3 minutes). Mix in bay leaf, chiles, broth, and tomato juice. Bring to a boil; then reduce heat, cover, and simmer for 20 minutes.

Grate 1 teaspoon peel from orange, then squeeze juice. Set grated peel and juice aside. Rinse fish fillets, pat dry, and cut into bite-sized pieces.

Add fish, orange peel, orange juice, and cilantro to simmering broth. Increase heat to medium, cover and simmer until fish is just slightly translucent; cut in thickest part to test (5-7 minutes). Season to taste with salt. Serve with lime wedges.

Serves 4

Gazpacho

12 ounces Roma tomatoes, crushed
1/2 cup green peppers, chopped
1/2 cup celery, chopped
1/2 cup cucumber, chopped
1/4 cup green onions, chopped
2 teaspoons fresh parsley
1 teaspoon snipped chives
2 cloves garlic, minced
3 tablespoons wine vinegar
1 teaspoon salt
1/4 teaspoon pepper
1 teaspoon Worcestershire sauce
1 large can tomato juice

Mix all ingredients and chill. Serve with dollop of sour cream.

Serves 4

Avocado Soup

6 cups beef or chicken stock
1 yellow onion, minced
1 tablespoon minced parsley
3 green chiles
2 medium avocados

Cook onion in stock until tender. Add parsley. Mash chiles with avocados, and top soup bowl with one tablespoon of this mixture just before serving. Delicious served with toasted tortillas.

Serves 6

Lime and Tortilla Soup

3 corn tortillas
2 cups vegetable oil
2 teaspoons vegetable oil
1/3 cup onion, chopped
1/4 cup canned green chiles, diced
4 cups chicken broth
1 cup shredded, cooked chicken (1 whole chicken breast)
1 tomato, chopped
1 tablespoon lime juice
4 large lime slices

Cut tortillas into 2-1/2 inch strips. Pour oil 1/2-inch deep in small skillet. Fry tortillas in hot oil until browned and crisp; drain on paper towels. Heat 2 tablespoons oil in large saucepan, add onions and chiles; sauté until onion is soft, but not browned. Add broth and chicken and bring to a boil. Cover and simmer for 20 minutes. Add tomato, simmer 5 minutes longer. Stir in lime juice. To serve: Ladle into bowl, add tortilla strips. Garnish with lime slices.

Serves 4

Gazpacho Salad

3 medium tomatoes, cut into wedges
1 medium cucumber, thinly sliced
1 medium green pepper, coarsely chopped
1 small red onion, thinly sliced
3 tablespoons cilantro
1/4 cup salad oil
3 tablespoons vinegar
1-1/2 teaspoons sugar
1 clove garlic, minced
1/4 tablespoon ground cumin
1/8 teaspoon dry mustard
1/8 teaspoon chili powder
3/4 teaspoon snipped fresh basil

In a mixing bowl combine tomatoes, cucumber, green pepper, onion, and cilantro. For dressing, in a screw-top jar combine oil, vinegar, sugar, garlic, basil, cumin, mustard, and chili powder. Cover and shake well. Pour over vegetable mixture, toss lightly to coat. Cover and chill for 2 or 3 hours, stirring occasionally. Transfer to a salad bowl. Garnish with avocado slices.

Serves 4

Calamari Fiesta

3 pounds calamari steak
1 quart chicken stock
1/2 cup lemon juice
1/4 cup lime juice
4 cloves garlic, pressed
1 red onion, thinly sliced
2 teaspoons ground cumin
1 bunch green onions, thinly sliced
1 yellow pepper, thinly sliced
1 bunch cilantro, coarsely chopped
1 tablespoon sugar
1 can water chestnuts, drained and thinly sliced
1 7-ounce can tomato paste

Rinse calamari well. Simmer the calamari in the chicken stock for 4 minutes. Remove from the stock and allow to cool on paper towels. Discard cooking liquid. Cut the calamari into 1/4-inch strips. In a large bowl combine all of the remaining ingredients. Add the calamari and toss well. Refrigerate tightly covered, overnight. Serve on a bed of greens and garnish with a slice of lime or serve with crackers or tortilla chips as an appetizer.

Serves 6

Ensalada Pollo y Garbanzo

2 cups cooked chicken or turkey, cubed
1 15-ounce can garbanzo beans, drained
1 cup Cheddar or Monterey Jack cheese, cubed
1 small bell pepper, chopped
2 green onions, chopped
1/2 cup mayonnaise
2 teaspoons lemon juice
1/2 tablespoon chili powder
1 clove garlic, minced
2 medium tomatoes, cut into wedges
2 tablespoons cilantro, minced
Lettuce leaves
1 avocado

In a medium bowl combine chicken, garbanzo beans, cheese, green pepper, and green onions. For dressing, stir together mayonnaise, lemon juice, chili powder, garlic, 1/4 teaspoon salt, 1/4 teaspoon pepper, and cilantro. Stir into chicken mixture. Cover and chill for 2-24 hours. Before serving, stir mixture. Serve on lettuce lined salad plates. Garnish with tomato wedges and avocado.

Serves 4

South of the Border Taco Salad

1 pound turkey or chicken, freshly ground
3 cloves garlic, minced
1 10-ounce can dark red kidney beans
1/4 cup yellow peppers, seeded and minced
1/2 cup tomato sauce
6 cups iceberg lettuce, torn
4 medium tomatoes, chopped
2 cups Montery Jack cheese, shredded
1 cup green pepper, chopped
1 avocado, sliced
4 green onions, sliced
1 cup black olives, sliced
4 tablespoons chili powder
6 tortilla cups

In a large skillet, cook meat, garlic, and yellow peppers. Add undrained beans, tomato sauce and chili powder. Bring to boil, reduce heat, and simmer covered for 10 minutes. Meanwhile, for salad, combine lettuce, tomatoes, cheese, green pepper, olives, and green onions. Add hot meat mixture, and toss. Divide among the tortilla cups and garnish with avocado. Serve with one of our salsas.

Serves 6

Tortilla Cups

In a heavy 3-quart saucepan, heat 2 inches of cooking oil. Place one 7-inch tortilla on top of the hot oil. Using a metal ladle, press tortilla into oil, forming the tortilla into a cup. Fry for 40-60 seconds, or until golden brown. Remove with tongs and drain on paper towel.

Serves 6

Mexican Seafood Salad

1 pound fresh crab meat
1/2 pound medium shrimp, peeled, deveined, and cooked
1/2 cup red onion, finely chopped
1/2 cup red and yellow pepper, sliced
1/2 cup scallions, sliced
1 ripe mango, cut into cubes
1/2 cup cilantro
1/2 cup pine nuts

Preheat oven to 300°. Spread pine nuts on a tray and toast for 10 minutes, or until browned. Cool and set aside. Toss remaining ingredients and chill. Use orange vinaigrette dressing or your favorite. Top with pine nuts.

Orange Vinaigrette Dressing

3/4 cup freshly squeezed orange juice
2 tablespoons freshly squeezed lime juice
1 tablespoon Dijon mustard
1 tablespoon ground cumin
2 tablespoons minced cilantro
1/4 cup olive oil
Salt and pepper to taste

Combine juices, mustard, cumin, cilantro, salt, and pepper. Beat constantly. Drizzle in olive oil.

Serves 4-6

Crab Fiesta

2 tablespoons salad oil
1 small onion, finely chopped
2 cloves garlic, minced or pressed
2 tablespoons paprika
1/2 tablespoon ground red pepper (cayenne)
1/2 tablespoon thyme
5 medium pear-shaped (Roma) tomatoes
   (about 1 pound), chopped
1 pound cooked crab meat
3 tablespoons lemon juice
1/3 cup fresh cilantro
2 green onions including tops, thinly sliced
Iceberg lettuce leaves, washed and crisped
Lemon wedges
Salt

Heat oil in a wide frying pan over medium heat. Add chopped onion and garlic. Cook, stirring often, until onion is tender, (4-5 minutes). Stir in paprika, red pepper, thyme, and half of the tomatoes. Cook, uncovered, stirring occasionally, until sauce is reduced to a thick pulp, (about 5 minutes). Remove from heat and stir in crab and lemon juice. Let cool (at least 30 minutes).

Stir in cilantro and about 1 cup of the remaining tomatoes; season to taste with salt. Line a platter with lettuce; spoon crab mixture on top. Garnish with remaining tomatoes and green onions. Serve with lemon wedges.

Serves 4

Shrimp Olé

6 slices white bread
1 pound small shrimp
1/2 pound Cheddar cheese
1/4 cup butter, melted
1/2 teaspoon dry mustard
3 whole eggs, beaten
1 pint milk
1 4-ounce can green chiles

Break bread and cheese in pieces about the size of a quarter. Arrange shrimp, bread, and cheese in several layers in greased casserole. Pour melted butter over the mixture. Beat eggs; add mustard, a dash of salt, and milk. Mix and pour over ingredients in casserole. Let stand minimum of 3 hours, preferably overnight in refrigerator, covered. Bake 2 hours, covered, at 350°.

Serves 6

Ceviche with Melon

8 ounces bay scallops, cut into 1/2-inch pieces
8 ounces small shrimp, deveined and halved lengthwise
8 ounces skinless, boneless white fish fillet,
   cut into small pieces
1 cup plus 3 tablespoons fresh lime juice
4 cups melon, cut into small pieces
1/2 scallion, thinly sliced
1/3 cup red pepper, chopped
1 cucumber, sliced
1/2 cup fruity olive oil
3 tablespoons red onion, sliced
1 clove garlic, chopped
1/2 teaspoon salt
1/4 teaspoon hot red pepper flakes
Salad greens
Sliced lime for garnish

Refrigerate all fish with the 1 cup of lime juice, covered overnight for at least 12 hours. 2 hours before serving, combine melon, scallion, red pepper, and cucumber in large bowl and refrigerate. Whisk oil, 3 tablespoons lime juice, onion, garlic, salt, and pepper flakes. Let stand at room temperature until flavors blend (about 30 minutes) Toss all together and serve on greens.

Serves 6 as first course or more as hors d'oeuvres

Santa Barbara Crab Enchiladas

6 corn tortillas
Vegetable oil
1-1/2 cups crabmeat
6 tablespoons onion, minced
Salsa con tomatillos
Shredded Monterey Jack cheese
Sour cream sauce (recipe below)

Heat tortillas one at a time in hot oil until soft. Place 1/4 cup crab meat in center of each tortilla and sprinkle with 1 tablespoon onion. Spread with a little Salsa con Tomatillos, roll up and place seam side down in 8 x 11-inch baking dish. Cover with remaining salsa. Sprinkle with cheese. Bake at 400° for 10 minutes until hot and cheese is melted. Serve with sour cream sauce.

Serves 4 to 6

Sour Cream Sauce

1/4 teaspoon garlic, minced
1/2 teaspoon salt
1 cup sour cream
2 tablespoons onion, chopped
2 tablespoons cilantro, chopped
2 tablespoons green chiles, chopped

Mash garlic with salt; combine with other ingredients. Add more chiles if you prefer sauce to be hotter.

Lamb Chili

4 large garlic cloves
2 jalapeño peppers
2 large onions, peeled and quartered
3-1/2 pounds boneless lamb shoulder,
   trimmed and cut into 1-inch cubes
Salt and coarsely ground pepper
2 tablespoons vegetable oil
1 4-ounce can green chili peppers, drained
2 tablespoons chili powder
2 tablespoons flour
1 tablespoon tomato paste
3 cups beef broth
2 medium zucchini, trimmed and cut to fit the feed tube
   vertically
1 pound can whole tomatoes, drained
1 tablespoon minced fresh oregano or 1 teaspoon dried

Drop the garlic and jalapeños through the feed tube of a food processor with the metal blade in place and the motor running and process until chopped finely, about 10 seconds. Reserve. Chop the onions coarsely in two batches. Sprinkle the lamb with 1 teaspoon salt and 1-1/2 teaspoons pepper. Heat the oil in a large stockpot over medium-high heat. Brown the lamb. Return the lamb to the pot, reduce the heat to moderate, and add the onions. Cook, stirring, until the onions are wilted and begin to color, about 5 minutes. Add the garlic, jalapeños, and chili peppers and cook, stirring for 3 minutes. Stir in the chili powder and flour and cook for 1 minute. Stir the tomato paste into the broth with a wire whisk until smooth. Add to the pot and bring to a boil. Reduce the heat and simmer, covered, until the lamb is tender, about 50 minutes, stirring occasionally. Slice the zucchini with the all-purpose slicing disc. Crush the tomatoes slightly and add to the pot with zucchini and oregano. Cook uncovered, until the zucchini is tender, about 5 minutes.

Serves 6-8

Pollo Verde

6 chicken breast halves, boned and skinned
2 cups chicken broth, divided
1/2 pound tomatillos
2 stalks celery, chopped
1 clove garlic, minced
1/2 medium onion, chopped
4 Anaheim chiles, roasted, peeled and chopped
1 bunch cilantro, stemmed and chopped

Poach chicken breasts in covered skillet with 1 cup chicken broth for 10 minutes. Combine all remaining ingredients in a saucepan and simmer for 20 minutes, purée, then simmer an additional 10 minutes. Correct seasonings. Pour over chicken in skillet and simmer, uncovered, 20 minutes or until chicken is done.

Serves 6

Serve with our salsa verde.

Mock Chili Rellenos

1 pound refried beans, canned
1 7-ounce sliced seeded whole green chiles, canned
1/2 pound cubed Jack cheese
2 eggs, separated
2 tablespoons flour
Salt and pepper

Spoon beans into a well-greased casserole. Press cheese cubes that have been wrapped in chili strips into the beans. Beat flour, salt, pepper, and egg yolks until thick. Beat egg whites until stiff, fold in yolk mixture and spoon over beans. Bake at 350° for 30 minutes. Serve with one of our salsas.

Serves 4-6 as a side dish

Chili Corn Soufflé

1/4 cup butter
1/4 cup flour
1 tablespoon salt
1/4 tablespoon black pepper
1/2 tablespoon paprika
1 cup milk
4 eggs, separated
1/2 can diced green chiles, drained
1 cup fresh ground corn kernels

Melt butter and blend in flour, salt, pepper, and paprika. Add milk and stir until well thickened. Beat egg yolks lightly and add small amount of hot sauce. Blend and return mixture to sauce. Cook, stirring a few minutes. Add chiles to sauce. Stir in corn. Beat egg whites until stiff, but still moist. Fold 1/3 of the egg whites into corn mixture, mixing well. Lightly fold in remaining egg whites. Turn into ungreased 1-quart soufflé dish. Place in a pan of hot water and bake at 350° for about 50 minutes.

Serves 6

Pan de Mexicana

1 pound can cream-style corn
3/4 cup milk
1/3 cup vegetable oil
2 eggs, slightly beaten
1 cup cornmeal
1/2 teaspoon baking soda
1 teaspoon salt
1/2 cup grated Cheddar cheese
1 4-ounce can chopped green chiles

Mix together the first four ingredients. Add cornmeal, baking soda and salt. Pour half the batter into greased 9 x 9-inch baking pan or round cake pan. Sprinkle with green chiles and half of the cheese. Spread remaining batter on top and sprinkle with remaining cheese. Bake 45 minutes at 400°. Cool just enough to set before cutting into squares or wedges.

Serves 8-10

Fideo

1 package coil vermicelli
15 ounces chicken broth
1 yellow onion, chopped
6 tomatoes, chopped
2 yellow chiles, seeds removed
2 cloves fresh garlic, minced
Salt and pepper to taste

Brown coil vermicelli in cooking oil until all vermicelli is a deep brown. Turn constantly. When vermicelli is browned, transfer to a pot. Add chicken broth, onion, tomatoes, seeded yellow chiles and garlic. Bring mixture to a boil. Cover and simmer for 1 hour, stirring occasionally to uncoil vermicelli. Uncover and simmer for 20 minutes, until mixture has thickened to desired consistency.

Serves 6

Holiday Hominy

1 15-ounce can hominy, drained
1 4-ounce can sliced olives, drained
1 4-ounce can chopped green chiles, drained
1 4-ounce jar sliced pimientos, drained
8 ounces sour cream
1/2 pound cubed Jack cheese
1/2 pound cubed Cheddar cheese
2 eggs, beaten
1 teaspoon Lawry's salt
1/2 teaspoons ground pepper

Fold all ingredients together and bake in a casserole dish at 350° for 45 minutes.

Serves 6-8

Lima Beans Mexicana

1 pound dry lima beans (soaked overnight)
2 cans ripe pitted sliced black olives
1 pound cheese (1/2 Monterey Jack, 1/2 Cheddar)
2 large onions, chopped
4 tablespoons bacon fat
1 pound ground round
4 tablespoons chili powder
4 tablespoons corn starch
1 teaspoon salt combined with 1 tablespoon
    dry mustard and water to make into paste

Soak beans overnight. Cook until done, not mushy. Strain and save liquid. Add approximately 4 tablespoons corn starch to thicken. Cook until thickened to gravy consistency. In 4 tablespoons bacon fat, sauté two chopped onions. Add 1 pound ground round. Sauté until crumbly. Mix beans, gravy, onion, meat and 3/4 of the cheese with chili powder and put in casserole. Add 1/4 cheese on top. Bake 45 minutes at 350°.

Serves 8 as a side dish

Santa Barbara Risotto

1 28-ounce can whole tomatoes,
  or 1-1/2 pounds fresh tomatoes
1 14-1/2 ounce can clear beef broth
2 tablespoons butter
1 cup converted rice
1 onion, coarsely chopped
1 clove garlic, crushed
1 16-ounce can pinto beans,
  drained—may add more if desired
1 4-ounce can diced green chiles
1-1/2 teaspoons chili powder
1 teaspoons cumin
Tabasco sauce to taste
1 medium zucchini, sliced
1 cup grated Jack cheese

Drain and coarsely chop tomatoes, reserving juice. Combine broth with enough juice to equal 2-1/2 cups; set aside. Melt butter in large skillet. Add rice, onion and garlic. Cook over medium-high heat, stirring frequently, 3-4 minutes, or until rice is translucent and onion is tender. Add combined liquids, tomatoes, beans, chiles, chili powder, cumin, and Tabasco sauce. Bring to a boil. Reduce heat. Cover tightly and simmer for 20 minutes. Remove from heat. Stir in zucchini. Let stand covered until all liquid is absorbed, about 5 minutes. Sprinkle with cheese.

Serves 6-8

Zucchini Pasilla

1-1/2 pounds small zucchini
2 yellow chiles, roasted, peeled, seeded
1 tablespoon lard or corn or safflower oil
8-ounce can tomatoes, drained
Salt to taste
2 eggs, separated
1/4 cup heavy cream
4-ounce Monterey Jack or natural cream cheese, thinly sliced
1 cup sour cream, mixed with salt to taste

Grate the zucchini, place in a colander, sprinkle with salt and allow to drain about 30 minutes, then squeeze the moisture from the zucchini by hand. Cut the chiles into thin strips and set aside. In heavy skillet, heat the lard or oil and add tomatoes along with chili strips; cook and stir over medium heat 3-4 minutes. Season to taste with salt. Remove the mixture from the heat and cool to room temperature. Beat the egg white until stiff; set aside. Beat the egg yolks until lemon colored. Mix together the egg yolks, zucchini, cream and the cooled tomato chili mixture. Fold in the beaten egg whites and pour into a heavily buttered 2-quart ovenproof dish. Bake in preheated 350° oven 30 minutes, or until set. Arrange the slices of cheese evenly over the top of the pudding and return the pudding to the oven for a few minutes until the cheese has slightly melted. Pour the sour cream over the pudding and serve at once.

Serves 4

Banana Empanadas

1-1/2 ounces unsalted butter
2 ounces nuts, finely chopped
1 tablespoon ground cinnamon
4 tablespoons sugar
4 large ripe bananas, sliced
4 flour tortillas, 9 inches diameter

Melt butter in heavy saucepan. Add nuts, cinnamon, sugar, and bananas. Sauté for 5 minutes. Cool; divide into four portions. Put one portion in center of each tortilla and roll, tucking in ends as for a burrito. Secure with toothpick. Heat light oil (corn or peanut) in a vessel for deep frying. Fry each empanada until golden brown and crisp. Cool slightly, then cut each into three portions and serve, topped with caramel sauce and a scoop of ice cream.

Serves 6

Caramel Sauce

1 cup sugar
1/2 cup water
1/2 teaspoon lime juice
1-1/2 ounces unsalted butter
8 ounces heavy cream

Mix sugar, water, and juice together in heavy pan. Cook over low heat until sugar is caramelized. Add cream and butter together slowly, whisking until thick. Pour over empanada.

Serves 6

Mexican Rice Flan

2 cups rice, uncooked
4 cups water
2-1/3 cups sugar
3 cups milk
1 can sweetened condensed milk
1/2 stick butter
2 teaspoons vanilla
1 cinnamon stick
3/4 cup raisins
1/2 teaspoon cinnamon
1/2 teaspoon nutmeg

Boil the rice with a cinnamon stick until all water is consumed. Add sugar, milk and condensed milk. Cook until half the milk is absorbed. Remove from heat and remove cinnamon stick. Grease individual ramekins with butter. Add raisins, butter, vanilla and spices to mixture. Sprinkle top with cinnamon and bake at 350° for 20 minutes.

Serves 8

Tortilla Torte

10 ounces semi-sweet chocolate
4-1/2 cups regular sour cream
3 tablespoons powdered sugar
1/2 teaspoon vanilla
1/4 teaspoon cinnamon
12 8-inch flour tortillas
Chocolate "leaves"

Melt chocolate over hot water in a double boiler and mix with 3-1/2 cups sour cream. Mix sugar and remaining sour cream, vanilla, and cinnamon and set aside. On a flat plate (large enough to hold tortillas) place two overlapping pieces of wax paper. (This is to keep the plate clean.) Layer eleven tortillas with the chocolate mixture. Add the twelfth tortilla and cover with sugar and sour cream mixture on top and sides. Refrigerate covered with a large bowl or other covering that does not touch the surface, for 12 hours. Decorate with chocolate leaves. Pull out wax paper on each side. To serve, cut with a very sharp knife into small wedges.

Chocolate Leaves

6 ounces semi-sweet chocolate
3 ounces milk chocolate
20 non-poisonous leaves (camellia, rose, etc.)

Melt chocolate. Generously spread CLEAN UNDERSIDE of leaves with chocolate. Refrigerate overnight. When ready to use, peel off leaf.

Note: this recipe is easy, quick, inexpensive, and gorgeous! It is always a conversation piece because of the tortillas and fits perfectly with a Mexican dinner. Serves many because it is rich.

Serves 12-15

Margarita

1 slice lime
Coarse kosher salt
1/2-ounce fresh lime juice
1/2-ounce fresh lemon juice
1/2-ounce tequila
1/2-ounce triple sec
4 ice cubes

Rub the inside of the chilled glass with the slice of lime and dip the glass into the salt. Combine all other ingredients in blender. Serve with garnish of slice of lime.

Serves 1

Sangria Blanca

1 bottle dry white wine
2 kiwis, peeled and sliced
1 large pear, sliced very thin
1 cup seedless green grapes
2 tablespoons super fine sugar
2 tablespoons Calvados or Armanac
3 tablespoons Cointreau
1-1/2 cups bottled sparkling water
Mint sprigs

Pour wine into large pitcher. Add fruits and liqueurs, cover and refrigerate 4-5 hours. Stir well, add sparkling water and pour over ice in tall glasses or in extra large wine glasses. Garnish with mint sprigs.

Serves 4-6

Sangria Negra

1/2 cup strongly brewed black tea (strained)
1 bottle dry red wine
Cherries, blackberries, black grapes
1 strip of lemon peel
1 strip of orange peel
Chilled club soda to taste

Place fruits and lemon and orange peel in large pitcher. Add tea and enough wine to cover. Chill remaining wine. Just before serving, pour remaining wine into pitcher. Stir, add ice and club soda to taste.

Serves 4-6

Seafood

Paella Valencia

1/3 cup olive oil
3 pounds frying chicken, cut into 8 pieces
Salt and pepper to taste
1 large onion, finely chopped
1 clove garlic, chopped
1-1/2 cups rice
Pinch saffron
2 cups chicken stock
1/2 cup tomatoes, peeled and chopped
12 unshelled clams, scrubbed
6 medium artichoke hearts, halved
12 shrimp, washed and shelled
2 Italian sausages

Heat the oil in a large skillet or paella pan and add the chicken. Brown the chicken well on both sides and season with salt and pepper. Remove chicken from the pan. Add onions and garlic and sauté. Add the rice and toss in the oil for several minutes until it turns yellow. Season with salt, pepper, and saffron. Pour enough stock to cover the rice, and let it cook down gently. Add chicken, tomatoes, artichokes, clams, shrimp, sausages, more stock, and water. Cook until rice is tender and the chicken is cooked.

Serves 6

Shrimp and Scallops in Tomato Cups

6-8 medium tomatoes
1/2 pound small scallops
3 tablespoons olive oil
1/2 pound small shrimp
1/2 cup bread crumbs
4 tablespoons butter
2 cloves garlic
1/2 cup parsley, minced
Pinch thyme
1 teaspoon lemon zest, grated
1/4 cup dry white vermouth
Parmesan cheese, freshly grated

Cut the tops off tomatoes and scoop out pulp. Sprinkle lightly with salt and turn upside down to drain. In small skillet, melt butter and stir in bread crumbs, garlic, parsley, thyme, and lemon zest. Set aside. In large skillet, heat olive oil, scallops, and shrimp and toss until they are heated through but not fully cooked. Add bread crumb mixture and toss to combine. Add vermouth. Cook over high heat tossing constantly for 2 minutes. Preheat oven to 425°. Fill tomatoes with mixture and sprinkle with Parmesan cheese. Bake 15 minutes. Sprinkle each tomato with chopped parsley and serve with lemon wedge.

Serves 6-8

Seafood Skewers
with Lemon-Thyme Butter

36 large shrimp, peeled, deveined with tails on
36 scallops
1/2 cup beer
1/2 cup olive oil
Juice of one orange
1 teaspoon thyme
1/2 teaspoon salt
Freshly ground pepper
1 stick sweet butter
2 tablespoons freshly chopped lemon thyme

Thread six skewers with alternating shrimp and scallops. Combine beer, olive oil, orange juice, thyme, salt, and pepper in a shallow dish and marinate seafood for 2 hours. Grill, basting and turning, approximately 5 minutes or until seafood is opaque. Blend butter and lemon thyme until smooth and melted.

Serves 6

Scallops with Sorrel and Mushrooms

2 pounds scallops
1/3 cup shallots, minced
3 tablespoons butter
1 tablespoon olive oil
1/4 cup mushrooms, sliced
1/4 cup dry vermouth
1 cup sorrel, shredded
1/2 cup heavy cream
Salt and pepper
Lemon juice

In a large skillet heat the butter and oil over moderate heat. Add shallots, scallops, mushrooms, sorrel, and vermouth and sauté for 2-3 minutes. Add cream, salt, pepper, and lemon juice to taste. Raise heat and cook until scallops are tender. Serve on bed of vermicelli.

Serves 6

Scallops with Vegetables

1 pound scallops
1/4 cup flour
Salt and pepper
Juice of 1/4 lemon
2 tablespoons butter
Garnish
    1 cup mushrooms, finely sliced
    1 cup green onions, chopped
    1 cup tomatoes, peeled and cut into eights
    2 ounces green pepper, finely sliced
    2 tablespoons parsley, chopped
    1 clove garlic, peeled and cut into fourths

Dry scallops, season, and dust with flour. Melt 1 tablespoon butter in a pan, add garlic. Add onions, reduce heat, and remove garlic pieces. Stir in green pepper and mushrooms and coat with butter. Stir in lemon and tomatoes. Season with salt and pepper. In a separate pan place enough butter to coat the bottom. Add scallops and sauté for 4 minutes, tossing them frequently. Add parsley. Serve on a platter topped with vegetable garnish.

Serves 4

Scallops, Tomatoes, and Hot Sausage Kabobs

24 scallops
24 cherry tomatoes
4 hot Italian sausages, cooked and cut into 6 slices each
1/2 stick melted butter
2 tablespoons olive oil
1 garlic clove, crushed
A splash Pernod
1/4 teaspoon crushed fennel seeds

Thread each of four skewers with alternating scallops, tomatoes, and sausage. Combine remaining ingredients and brush kabobs, covering thoroughly. Grill, turning and basting for approximately 5 minutes.

Serves 4

Perfect Scampi

2 pounds large shrimp (18-24 count)
1/2 stick sweet butter
2 tablespoons olive oil
2 large garlic cloves, minced
1/4 cup minced fresh parsley
1 teaspoon fresh basil
1/4 cup dry vermouth
Salt and pepper

Peel and devein shrimp. In a skillet large enough to hold all of the shrimp, heat butter and olive oil over high heat. When it is foamy and hot add the shrimp and toss to coat. Add remaining ingredients and continue to turn and toss shrimp for 3-4 minutes, or until they turn pink and have just changed from translucent to opaque. Serve immediately with pan juices and sprinkle with more parsley. Garnish with lemon wedges. Good served with pasta.

Serves 4

Greek Shrimp

1 onion, diced
2 tablespoons butter
1-1/2 tablespoons olive oil
1/2 cup white wine
4-5 small tomatoes, chopped
2 tablespoons fresh garlic, minced
Salt and pepper
1/2 teaspoon oregano
4-5 ounces crumbled feta cheese
2 pounds raw large shrimp, shelled and deveined
6 fresh basil leaves, torn into pieces

In a heavy skillet, heat oil and butter. Add onion, wine, garlic, salt, and pepper, oregano and basil. Sauté. Once onions are tender, add tomatoes. Simmer until tomatoes are heated thoroughly. Add shrimp, cover and simmer until shrimp are pink. Top with feta cheese. Broil until cheese browns. Serve immediately.

Serves 4-6

Shrimp au Gratin with Dill

1 pound fresh medium shrimp, cooked
1/4 cup butter
1/2 pound fresh mushrooms, sliced
2 tablespoons chopped green onions
1/4 cup flour
1/2 teaspoon pepper
1 clove garlic, crushed
3/4 teaspoon dried or fresh dill weed
1 cup milk
2/3 cup white cooking wine
1/2 cup seasoned bread crumbs
6-8 ounces sharp Cheddar cheese, shredded

Sauté mushrooms, green onions, and garlic in butter for 5 minutes. Stir in flour, pepper, dill, and milk. Bring to a boil, stirring often. Remove from heat and add one half of the cheese. Stir until melted. Add wine. Combine the shrimp, mushroom sauce and remaining cheese. Mix lightly. Pour into casserole. Sprinkle crumbs on top. Dot with butter. Bake at 375° until brown and bubbly, about 20-30 minutes. Serve over rice or linguini noodles. Garnish with parsley.

Serves 4

Fettuccine and Mussels in Cilantro Butter

32 mussels, scrubbed and debearded
1 teaspoon salt
7 ounces red bell pepper, cut into 1/4-inch strips
1 cup pecans, toasted and chopped
1/2 cup cilantro leaves
1/2 cup fresh parsley
1 clove garlic
1 jalapeño chili
1/2 cup butter, chilled and cut into 8 pieces
1 teaspoon fresh lime juice
1/2 teaspoon salt
6 ounces fettucine, cooked

Combine mussels and 1 teaspoon salt in large saucepan. Add enough cold water to cover. Let soak 30 minutes, then drain. Return mussels to saucepan, cover and cook 6 minutes. Discard any mussels that do not open. Cool and remove mussels from shells. Discard shells. Combine cilantro and parsley in bowl. With food processor, mince garlic and chili. Drop butter into processor and process 10 seconds. Add lime juice and salt and blend 10 seconds. Transfer butter mixture to 12-inch skillet and melt over medium heat. Add fettucine and mussels and toss to coat. Cook about 6 minutes to heat through. Remove from heat and mix in bell pepper and reserved nuts.

Serves 4

Mussels with Broth

1 large onion, chopped
1/4 cup sweet butter
3 cups chicken stock
2 cups white wine or dry vermouth
3 pounds fresh mussels, scrubbed and debearded
Salt
1/2 cup butter
4 cloves garlic

Sauté onions in butter until transparent. In large shallow pan, add stock, wine, garlic, and chopped parsley. Simmer 1 hour, uncovered. Strain broth and return to pan. Add cleaned, scrubbed mussels and cook until mussels open. Remove mussels to serving bowls. Continue to simmer broth and whisk in 1/2 cup butter and add salt to taste. Serve with French bread for dunking.

Serves 8-12

Baked Oysters Somerset

6 oysters, fresh in shell
2 teaspoons garlic, minced
1 teaspoon shallots, minced
2 tablespoons butter
Pepper to taste
Nutmeg to taste
3 teaspoons Romano cheese, grated
2 teaspoons parsley, chopped
2 tablespoons oyster crackers, crumbled
1 lemon wedge

In food processor chop crackers and remaining ingredients, except oysters. Open oysters. Leave in half shell. Cover oysters with 1 teaspoon of paste. Top with 1/2 teaspoon cheese. Bake in preheated oven at 450° for 10-15 minutes.

Serves 1, can be multiplied by any amount

Rex Sole in Saffron and Tomato Sauce

6 whole sole
Milk
Flour
1/3 stick butter
2 tomatoes, peeled, seeded, and chopped
1 clove garlic, minced
1/4 cup dry white wine
Pinch saffron
Salt and pepper
Lemon juice

Make several diagonal slashes on either side of sole. Dip each fish in milk and then in flour. Heat butter in skillet over high heat and add fish. Turn fish over after about 3 minutes. Add tomatoes, scallions, garlic, wine, saffron, lemon juice, salt, and pepper and lower heat to simmer until fish is opaque. Remove fish to platter and keep warm. Cook sauce until reduced, pour over fish and serve immediately.

Serves 6

Piquant Baked Fish

2 pounds fillet of halibut, white sea bass or mahi mahi
2 cups sauterne or dry white wine
1 tablespoon salt
1 to 1-1/2 cups fine dry bread crumbs
2 eggs
1 cup mayonnaise
1 cup sour cream
1 cup sliced almonds, slightly browned
Paprika as garnish
1/4 cup chopped onion

Combine wine, salt, and serving size fish pieces in a shallow glass pan. Marinate for at least 2 hours or overnight. Drain fish thoroughly on paper towels. Beat the eggs. Dip fish into egg and then into bread crumbs to coat. Arrange fish pieces one layer deep in shallow baking dish with a space between each piece. Blend mayonnaise, sour cream, onion, and 3/4 cup of almonds. Spread this mixture over each piece, letting it cover the sides also. Sprinkle any extra crumbs and the remaining almonds on top. Dust with paprika. Bake at 425° for 15-20 minutes. Serve immediately.

Serves 6-8

Trout with Sorrel Butter

6 rainbow trout, boned
2 cups sorrel leaves
6 tablespoons melted butter
Sliced lemon
Salt and pepper

Season inside of fish with salt, and pepper. Place sorrel leaves in cavity. Brush outside of fish with butter, salt and pepper. Place 2 slices of lemon on top of each fish. Wrap each fish in a double thick foil and grill about 10 minutes, turning once.

Serves 6

Poached Whole Fish
with Garden Vegetables

4 pounds whole fish, not fillets
1 large onion, sliced
2 cups celery, chopped
1/2 cup green pepper, chopped
3 tablespoons olive oil
5 medium tomatoes, chopped
1 cup vermouth
1/4 cup fresh lime juice
8 cloves garlic
1 teaspoon oregano, crushed
1/2 teaspoon thyme, crushed
1 medium bay leaf, crushed
4 tablespoons fresh parsley, chopped
2 teaspoons mild chili powder
Tabasco to taste

Sauce: Sauté onion, celery, and green pepper in oil until browned. Add remaining ingredients, except fish, and simmer for 10 minutes.

Prepare: Cover fish with milk and keep in refrigerator while preparing sauce. Remove fish from milk and rinse well. Pat dry. Mix 1 cup of flour with 1-1/2 teaspoons fresh ground pepper. Dredge fish inside and out with the seasoned flour. Place fish in baking dish on rack and pour sauce over and around. Baste frequently. Bake in 350° oven uncovered for 20-30 minutes, until fish is opaque.

Serves 4

Poached Salmon
and Asparagus on Fettuccine

1/2 pound asparagus, trimmed
3-1/2 cups dry white wine
6 shallots, minced
4 (6 to 8 ounce) salmon fillets, cut 1 inch thick
3 tablespoons whipping cream
2 cups butter, cut into small pieces
2 teaspoons fresh lemon juice
1 teaspoon lemon peel, freshly grated
Fresh chives, snipped
Salt and pepper
1 pound fresh fettuccine
1/2 cup whipping cream
Salt and pepper

Cook asparagus in large pot of boiling salted water until crisp, about 5 minutes. Drain and pat dry. Reserve. Boil 2-1/2 cups wine and shallots in heavy medium saucepan until liquid is reduced to 2 tablespoons. Set aside. Preheat oven to 450°. Arrange salmon skin-side down in flameproof baking dish. Pour remaining 1 cup wine over salmon. Bring to boil. Turn fish over. Cover with parchment or foil. Cook until opaque, 4-5 minutes. Meanwhile, whisk cream into wine and shallot mixture. Set pan over low heat and whisk in butter one piece at a time, removing pan from heat briefly if drops of melted butter appear. If sauce breaks down at any time, remove from heat and whisk in 2 tablespoons cold butter. Blend in lemon juice, peel, and chives. Season with salt and pepper. Keep warm in top of double boiler over hot water. Cook pasta in large pot of boiling water. Drain and transfer to a bowl. Mix in cream and season to taste. Arrange mounds of fettuccine on both sides of plate. Place salmon in-between mounds. Arrange asparagus in criss-cross pattern atop salmon. Surround salmon with sauce and serve.

Serves 4

Grilled Salmon Steaks
with Mustard-Thyme Hollandaise

6 salmon steaks
Olive oil
Salt and pepper
3 egg yolks
1 tablespoon water
2 sticks sweet butter
Salt and pepper
1-2 tablespoons lemon juice
1-1/2 teaspoons Dijon mustard
1/4 teaspoon thyme

Prepare hollandaise sauce first. Combine egg yolks and water in heavy saucepan. Over low heat or in double boiler, whisk egg yolks and water and add butter slowly in small pieces, whisking all the time to keep sauce from separating. Remove from heat and add salt, pepper, lemon juice, mustard, and thyme. Rub salmon steaks with olive oil and season with salt and pepper. Grill 4-5 minutes per side. Serve with hollandaise sauce on the side.

Serves 6

Calamari Putanesca

1 stick unsalted butter
2 tablespoons parsley, minced
3 teaspoons garlic, minced
3 tablespoons shallots, minced
2 teaspoons Dijon mustard
4 anchovy fillets, minced
3 tablespoons brandy
1/2 teaspoon cayenne
2-1/2 pounds squid, cleaned
4 tablespoons olive oil
2 tablespoons flour
2 tablespoons black olives, chopped
3 teaspoons capers
2 cups tomatoes, finely chopped and seeded
1/3 cup lemon juice
1-1/3 cups dry white wine

Make a sauce with the butter, 1 teaspoon garlic, cayenne pepper, shallots, parsley, mustard, anchovies, and 2 tablespoons of brandy. Cook over low heat, stirring occasionally for 5 minutes. Remove from heat.

Clean and cut the squid into 1/2-inch rings, pat dry and toss with the flour. Heat the olive oil and cook the squid quickly over high heat, stirring for 1-2 minutes or until the squid is white. Remove squid and keep warm. Drain all but 1 tablespoon oil and add 2 teaspoons of the garlic and sauté over medium heat for about 1 minute. Add the olives and capers and cook 30 seconds. Stir in the lemon juice, white wine, 1 tablespoon of brandy, and cook 1 additional minute. Stir in the sauce, squid, and fresh tomatoes and cook until heated through.

Serves 8

Poultry

Poached Chicken Breast
with Artichoke Hearts

1 cup chicken broth
1 can artichoke hearts (not marinated)
4 tablespoons butter
1/4 cup flour
3/4 cup milk
1/2 cup Parmesan cheese
2 tablespoons sherry
1/2 teaspoon rosemary
1/4 pound mushrooms
4 chicken breasts
Salt and pepper to taste

Preheat oven to 325°. Poach breasts in broth in shallow skillet until tender. Save broth. Cool, skin, and bone. Arrange chicken in a small, shallow casserole. Sauté mushrooms in 1/4 cup of broth. Distribute mushrooms and artichoke heart pieces over chicken. Melt 4 tablespoons butter in skillet. Stir in flour, salt, pepper, 3/4 cup chicken broth, and milk. Cook until thickened. Add grated Parmesan cheese, sherry and rosemary. Pour over chicken. Bake uncovered for 30 minutes.

Serve over rice or noodles.

Serves 4

Lemon-Walnut Chicken

6 chicken breasts, boned and skinned
4 tablespoons butter
1-2 eggs, beaten
1/2 cup flour
Sauce
4 tablespoons butter
2 cloves of garlic, minced
2 tablespoons shallots, minced
2 tablespoons flour
1-1/2 cups chicken stock
1/2 cup Marsala wine (dry)
1/4 cup fresh lemon juice
1/2 cup chopped and toasted walnuts
Parsley, garnish
Lemon slices, garnish

FOR CHICKEN: Season the chicken breasts with salt and pepper. Heat butter in skillet. Dredge each chicken piece in flour and shake off excess. Dip chicken in beaten eggs and sauté until golden on both sides. Drain on paper towels.

FOR SAUCE: Melt butter in 1-quart saucepan. Add garlic and shallots and sauté for 1 minute. Add flour, stirring constantly. Do not allow mixture to brown. Add stock and Marsala and continue to stir until smooth and slightly thickened. Add lemon juice. (Can be prepared 1-2 hours ahead to this point). Preheat oven to 375°. Place drained chicken pieces in baking dish. Pour sauce over chicken and bake until tender, about 20-30 minutes. When ready to serve, sprinkle with chopped walnuts, parsley, and lemon slices.

Serves 6

Chicken Adobo

1 chicken, cut up
Salt and pepper
1/2 cup white vinegar
4 large cloves garlic, peeled
3 tablespoons oil
1 onion, sliced
1 can pickling spice, tied in cheesecloth bag
1/2 cup tomato sauce
1/4 cup soy sauce

Rinse and dry chicken pieces. Season with salt and pepper, place in bowl with vinegar, and rub well. Heat oil in Dutch oven. Crush garlic and sauté in oil until dark brown, then remove and discard garlic. Sauté onion in garlic oil. Add chicken and vinegar, stir well, cover, and simmer over medium heat for 10 minutes. Add pickling spices, cover, and simmer 10 minutes. Add tomato and soy sauce, cover, and simmer about 20 minutes, stirring occasionally, until chicken is tender.

Serve over rice.

Serves 4

Chicken with Tomatoes in Tarragon Sauce

8 mushrooms
3 shallots
1 14-ounce can whole peeled tomatoes
1 chicken, cut up
3 tablespoons butter
1/2 cup dry white wine
1 tablespoon fresh tarragon or 1 teaspoon dried tarragon
1/4 teaspoon dried thyme
1/2 cup heavy cream
2 cups cooked rice, hot

Slice mushrooms and shallots. Chop the tomatoes. Melt 2 tablespoons butter in large skillet. Cover and cook the chicken in one layer, turning occasionally until brown, about 10 minutes. Cover and cook 25 minutes longer.

While chicken is cooking, melt 1 tablespoon butter in small pan and add sliced mushrooms. Cook for 3 minutes.

Transfer cooked chicken to a platter and keep warm while preparing the sauce.

Degrease the skillet, leaving only pan juices. Add shallots and cook for 30 seconds. Add wine, tomatoes, mushrooms, tarragon, and thyme to skillet. Cook 5 minutes over high heat to reduce sauce. Lower the heat and stir in the cream, and cook 2 minutes. Place rice on individual plates with chicken nestled in the middle and cover with the sauce.

Serves 4

Tarragon Chicken

4 whole chicken breasts (boned)
2 tablespoons flour
1/4 cup butter
1-1/2 tablespoons shallots or green onion
    (white part only)
1/2 cup dry white wine
1/2 cup chicken broth
1-1/2 teaspoons dry tarragon
1/2 cup whipping cream
Salt and pepper to taste

Skin and bone chicken breasts. Chop shallots. Season breasts with salt and pepper and sauté them in 3 tablespoons butter for 2 minutes on each side. Transfer to plate. Sauté shallots in butter 2 minutes. Add wine and reduce liquid to about 1/2 cup, add flour and mix to a paste. Now add chicken broth and tarragon, return chicken to pan and cover. Cook on low heat for approximately 20 minutes. Add cream and remaining 1 tablespoon of butter and warm.

Place chicken on the center of a large platter and pour sauce over it. Serve with accompanying vegetables along both sides of platter.

Serves 4

Polla alla Bolognese

8 chicken breasts, boned
1/4 cup flour
1 teaspoon salt
Fresh ground pepper, to taste
4 tablespoons butter
8 slices Prosciutto
8 slices Fontina or bel paese cheese, thinly sliced
1/2 cup chicken broth
1 tablespoon brandy

Preheat oven to 350°. Place each chicken breast between two sheets of wax paper and pound until 1/4 inch thick. Sprinkle each chicken breast with salt and pepper. Dredge in flour. Heat butter in heavy skillet. Sauté breasts over low heat 2-3 minutes. Do not over cook. Remove to shallow 2-quart glass baking dish. On each piece of chicken arrange a slice of Prosciutto and a slice of cheese. Into the brown juices of the skillet stir the wine, chicken broth and brandy. Simmer until liquid is reduced and slightly thickened, about 5 minutes. Pour over the chicken breast. Bake uncovered until hot and bubbly, about 15 minutes.

Serves 8

Chicken Breasts in Orange Sauce

6 chicken breast halves, skinned
1/2 teaspoon cinnamon
2 tablespoons ginger
1/2 teaspoon pepper
3 tablespoons leeks
1 6-ounce can orange juice (concentrated)
2 tablespoons soy sauce
3 cloves garlic
2 tablespoons cornstarch in 1 tablespoon water
1/2 teaspoon salt
1/4 teaspoon dry mustard
2 tablespoons butter or olive oil
2 tablespoons sugar

Preheat oven to 350°. Sauté the chicken in oil or butter with the leeks and garlic. Sprinkle with salt and pepper and cook for 10 minutes. Put the chicken in a baking pan. In a bowl mix the soy sauce, sugar, ginger, mustard, cinnamon, and orange juice. Pour over the chicken and bake for 30 minutes. Drain sauce from pan and add the cornstarch and water to make sauce. Cook until thickened (5-10 minutes). Serve over angel hair pasta or rice.

Serves 6

Chicken Wrapped in Prosciutto
Pollo al Prosciutto

1 2-pound chicken, cut up
3 tablespoons sweet butter
5 large sage leaves, fresh
1 teaspoon rosemary leaves, fresh
1 teaspoon dried marjoram
1 teaspoon salt
1/4 teaspoon black pepper, freshly ground
1 tablespoon olive oil
8 slices Prosciutto (about 1/2 pound)

Melt the butter in a small saucepan. Finely chop the sage, rosemary, and marjoram. Put the chopped ingredients into a small bowl. Add the melted butter and the salt and pepper to the chopped ingredients. Mix.

Lay a large sheet of aluminum foil on the table and brush the shiny side with the oil. Use a pastry brush to coat each piece of chicken with the herb-butter mixture.

Wrap each piece in a slice of Prosciutto. Place the chicken pieces on the aluminum foil, fitting the whole chicken back together again.

Wrap the chicken the way you make a package. Place the package in a terra-cotta casserole and cover.

Bake for 1 hour and 45 minutes at 450° without opening the casserole. Remove the casserole from the oven and let stand for 5 minutes, then remove the lid. Use scissors to cut from the center of the foil outward in all four directions. Then cut each foil quarter in half.

Fold back each of the foil pieces from the center to the side of the casserole, making a flower shape.

Serve immediately.

Serves 4

Kung Pao Chicken

2 whole chicken breasts, skinned, boned, and
   cut into about 1/2 inch cubes
   (about 1 to 1-1/2 pounds total)
1 whole green bell pepper, seeded, cut into cubes
4 whole scallions, cut into about 1-inch diagonal lengths
1 cup peanuts, raw and shelled
1 cup peanut or corn oil
Sesame oil/hot chili oil for stir frying

MARINADE

1 tablespoon light soy
1 tablespoon Shaohsing or sherry
1/2 teaspoon sugar
1/2 teaspoon sesame or peanut oil
1 tablespoon cornstarch
Dash of salt

AROMATICS

8 dried red chili peppers (cut off stem end
   and remove seeds)
4 cloves garlic, minced
4 quarter-sized slices fresh ginger, minced

SEASONING SAUCE

1 tablespoon hoisin sauce
2 tablespoons light soy sauce
2 tablespoons Shaohsing or sherry
1 tablespoon red wine vinegar or rice vinegar
1/4 tablespoon Sichuan peppercorns
    (roasted and ground)

BINDER

1 tablespoon cornstarch mixed with
2 tablespoons cold water

Combine the marinade ingredients except the oil and cornstarch with the chicken. When well combined, sprinkle the chicken mixture with the cornstarch, recombine, then add the oil and mix again. The chicken should have a light sheen. Set aside for at least 15-30 minutes.

Prepare aromatics and set aside in individual containers.

Prepare seasoning sauce and binder and set aside.

Heat one cup of peanut or corn oil to 375° and roast peanuts. Prepare proper straining equipment prior to cooking—as soon as the peanuts begin to take on color, they must be removed from the oil. They continue to cook even after removal. Set drained nuts aside.

Heat a wok until hot, add 2 tablespoons peanut oil, add chili peppers, remove when they have browned (reserve), and add chicken. Stir fry chicken until browned and remove from wok to a warm serving plate.

Return wok to heat. When hot, add 1-2 tablespoons oil, then garlic and ginger. When these aromatics are lightly golden, add bell pepper and scallion; after a few seconds, return chicken and peppers to the wok and combine with other ingredients.

Add seasoning sauce in small amounts around the sides of the wok. Thicken with the binder to a glaze consistency. Turn off heat, adjust seasonings, salt, sesame oil, chili oil, and add peanuts. Combine and serve immediately.

Serves 4

Grilled Ginger-Sesame Chicken Marinade

1/2 cup olive oil
1/2 cup white wine
1/2 cup soy sauce
2 tablespoons ginger, grated
1 tablespoon dry mustard
1 teaspoon pepper
4 cloves garlic, crushed
1/2 cup green onion, chopped
3 tablespoons sesame seeds
8 chicken breasts

Combine all marinade ingredients and marinate in bowl in refrigerator for 6-8 hours. Remove and reserve marinade. Grill chicken for 20 minutes and baste with marinade.

Serves 8

Thyme and Soy Marinade

4 chicken breast, boned
1/2 cup olive oil
4 tablespoons soy sauce
2 tablespoons thyme,
    fresh or 1-1/2 teaspoons dried

Place chicken breasts in bowl. Cover with oil, soy sauce, and thyme. Marinate for 1 hour. Grill or broil chicken and use sauce for basting.

Serves 4

Lime and Vegetable Chicken

2 whole chickens
2 large limes
4 medium garlic cloves, minced
2 teaspoons salt
1 teaspoon pepper, ground
1 tablespoon oregano, dried
1/4 cup olive oil
1 medium onion
6 carrots
6 celery ribs
4 medium potatoes
2/3 cup fresh lime juice
2/3 cup chicken broth

Rinse chickens and pat dry. Pierce limes at 1/4 inch intervals with a two-prong fork. Place lime in cavity of each chicken.

Mince garlic and put into small mixing bowl. Add salt, pepper, oregano and 1/4 cup olive oil. Mix. Rub onto chickens reserving a small amount.

Chop onion, celery, and carrots and cube and peel potatoes into 2-inch cubes. Place vegetables on the bottom of a large roasting pan. Place chickens on top. Stir together lime juice and chicken broth in remaining mixing bowl sauce. Pour over chickens and vegetables.

Bake uncovered in 450° oven for 20 minutes with breast side up. Turn chicken over for next 20 minutes, then turn breast side up for last 20 minutes, basting often.

Remove limes from chicken cavities and quarter the chicken, serving with arranged vegetables on platter. Degrease pan juices and serve as sauce.

Serves 8

Apricot Chicken

4 chicken breasts, boned and skinned
30 ounces apricot halves, well drained, reserve juice
1/2 cup almonds, blanched, toasted, and slivered
1/4 teaspoon nutmeg
1/2 teaspoon cinnamon
2 tablespoons seasoned bread crumbs
3 tablespoons brown sugar
1 cup dry vermouth
5 tablespoons butter or margarine
1/4 cup lemon or lime juice
1 tablespoon cornstarch

Place each chicken breast between two sheets of waxed paper and pound until 1/4 inch thick.

To prepare stuffing, chop one half of the apricots coarsely. Combine the chopped apricots with the almonds, nutmeg, cinnamon, bread crumbs, 1 tablespoon brown sugar, and 2 tablespoons vermouth. Divide the stuffing evenly between the chicken breasts. Place stuffing in a line in the center of each breast. Place 1/2 tablespoon butter on top of stuffing before rolling each breast tightly and securing with a toothpick or a piece of string at each end.

Melt remaining butter in a frying pan. Brown chicken rolls on all sides. Add remaining vermouth, lime juice, and remaining 2 tablespoons brown sugar to the pan and simmer covered for 25 minutes or until chicken is tender. Add remaining apricot halves to sauce to heat through. Stir corn starch in 1/4 cup reserved apricot juice and stir into sauce. Continue to heat and stir until thickened. Place chicken rolls in center of serving platter and top with sauce.

Serves 4

Chicken And Crabmeat Casserole

1/4 to 1/2 cup butter
7 tablespoons flour
1-1/2 cups chicken broth
3/4 teaspoon paprika
3/4 teaspoon salt
1/2 cup white wine
Parsley
2-1/4 cups sour cream
2 cans (7 1/2 ounces each) crabmeat or use
    Wakefield frozen or fresh*
3 cups cooked, diced chicken*
1 cup bread crumbs
2 tablespoons melted butter
Sautéed sliced mushrooms

Melt 1/4 cup butter and blend in flour. Add broth, wine and seasonings. Cook until thick and smooth. Blend in sour cream, crabmeat, chicken and mushrooms. Place in casserole. Sprinkle breadcrumbs on top. Bake at 350° for 25 minutes.

* More crabmeat and chicken may be added if you prefer.

Serves 8

Chicken Provençal

1 chicken, 3-1/2 pounds, cut into 10 serving pieces
1/2 cup flour
Salt and freshly ground pepper to taste
2 tablespoons olive oil
4 sprigs fresh thyme or 1 teaspoon dried
2 teaspoons chopped fresh rosemary or 1 teaspoon dried
2 teaspoons chopped fresh oregano or 1/2 teaspoon dried
12 cloves garlic, unpeeled
1 bay leaf
1/2 cup dry white wine
1/2 cup chicken broth
2 tablespoons butter
1/4 cup fresh chopped chervil or 1/4 cup chopped parsley

Dredge the chicken pieces in flour seasoned with salt and pepper. Heat 1 tablespoon of the olive oil in a nonstick skillet over medium high heat and add the chicken pieces skin side down. Cook 4-5 minutes until golden brown. Turn the chicken and cook until golden brown on the other side, about 3 minutes. Pour off the fat and add the remaining 1 tablespoon oil, thyme, rosemary, oregano, garlic cloves, and bay leaf. Cook, shaking the skillet and stirring the chicken pieces so that the herbs are evenly distributed. Cook about 3 minutes. Add the wine and bring to a simmer, scraping the bottom of the skillet and stirring briefly. Cook until reduced by half. Add the chicken broth and simmer. Cover and cook about 10 minutes. The sauce should be reduced by half. Remove the bay leaf. Swirl in the butter. Sprinkle the chervil over all and serve with the garlic cloves.

Serves 4

Chinese Chicken

1 whole chicken, cut up
1 tablespoon oil
1/3 cup soy sauce
1/3 cup brown sugar
1/2 cup water
1 tablespoon ketchup
1/4 cup apple juice
1 clove garlic, crushed
1 green onion, sliced
2 tablespoons cornstarch
1 tablespoon water
2 tablespoons sesame seeds

In skillet, brown chicken pieces in oil. Mix together the soy sauce, brown sugar, water, ketchup, apple juice, garlic, and green onion and pour over the chicken in skillet. Simmer 35-45 minutes. Drain fat from sauce. Add cornstarch and water to pan sauces until thick. Pour sauce over chicken and garnish with sesame seeds. Serve with white rice.

Serves 4-6

Tarragon Marinated Chicken

6 chicken thighs
6 chicken breasts, boned
2 cloves garlic, smashed
1/2 cup olive oil
Juice of 1/2 lemon
1/4 cup white wine
1 teaspoon pepper, ground
1 teaspoon salt
3 tablespoons tarragon, fresh and finely chopped
   or 1 tablespoon crushed dried tarragon

Combine all ingredients in a large bowl. Marinate in refrigerator for 24 hours. Barbecue over medium-hot coals.

Serves 6

Turkey-Rice Salad

1 cup packaged quick brown rice
1/4 teaspoon salt
1-1/4 cups boiling water
1 cup sliced mushrooms
2 tablespoons butter
3 tablespoons pine nuts, toasted
6 slices bacon, cooked, crumbled
2 turkey thighs, skinned, boned
2 bunches spinach, cleaned
3 medium tomatoes, cut into wedges

Stir rice and salt into boiling water. Reduce heat to low, cover tightly and simmer 12-14 minutes. Sauté mushrooms in 1 tablespoon butter until soft: combine with rice, pine nuts, and bacon.

Brown thighs in remaining 1 tablespoon butter; add 1 tablespoon of balsamic vinaigrette (see below). Cover and cook until tender, about 15-20 minutes or until done; slice thinly. For each salad, top spinach and tomatoes with rice mixture and warm sliced turkey. Drizzle each with balsamic vinaigrette.

Serves 4

Balsamic Vinaigrette

3 tablespoons balsamic vinegar
2 tablespoons chopped shallots
2 tablespoonsfresh marjoram, chopped or 1 teaspoon, dried
1/2 cup olive oil

Combine vinegar, shallots, and marjoram; slowly pour in oil while whisking.

Roast Duck with Green Grapes

1 5-pound duck
Salt and pepper
Thyme
Bay leaf
2 tablespoons red wine vinegar
1/2 cup beef broth
1/4 cup dry vermouth
Splash cognac
1 cup seedless grapes

Preheat oven to 450°. Season inside of duck with salt, pepper, thyme, and bay leaf. Prick skin of duck. Place on roasting rack in shallow roasting pan. Roast 35 minutes, basting every 15 minutes, and draining fat while cooking. Roast for a total of 1-1/2 hours. Remove all but 2 tablespoons of fat from pan, add vinegar, beef broth, vermouth, and cognac and reduce slightly. Add grapes, carve duck, and serve with sauce.

Serves 4

Sautéed Game Hens
in Spicy Sauce

3 game hens, halved
1/2 cup olive oil
Salt and pepper
1 bunch green onions, finely chopped
1/2 cup beef stock
1/4 cup dry red wine
1/2 teaspoon dry mustard
1 tablespoon red wine vinegar
1 teaspoon Worcestershire sauce
2 teaspoons butter

Heat oil in heavy skillet, brown seasoned hens and cook for 10 minutes. Add green onions, beef stock, and wine. Lower heat and simmer until hens are tender, about 20 minutes. Remove hens to serving platter and keep warm. Skim off fat and add to remaining pan juices the dry mustard, vinegar, and Worcestershire sauce. Raise the heat and boil for a few minutes to reduce. Turn off heat and stir in butter. Pour sauce over hens.

Serves 6

Roast Duck with Green Peppercorns

2 ducks (4-1/2 to 5 pounds each)
Salt, paprika
2 tablespoons green peppercorns, mashed
1 orange, quartered
2 tablespoons butter
3 tablespoons shallots
2 tablespoons brandy
1/2 cup brown sauce
3 tablespoons green peppercorns, mashed
1 cup heavy cream
1-1/2 tablespoons minced parsley
1/4 teaspoon tarragon

Season ducks inside and out with salt and paprika. Spread mashed peppercorns on outside of ducks. Fill body cavities with orange quarters and skewer shut. Roast in 425° oven for 25 minutes. Pierce skin to release fat. Melt butter in skillet. Sauté shallots, add brandy, brown sauce (1 cup beef bouillon, 2 tablespoons butter, 2 tablespoons flour), and crushed peppercorns. Bring to boil, add cream and boil again. Stir in minced parsley and tarragon. Serve sauce to accompany carved duck.

Serves 8

Quail with Olives and Wild Mushrooms

12 quail
4 slices lean bacon
2 tablespoons butter
Flour for dusting quails
Salt and pepper
8 crushed juniper berries
1/2 teaspoon thyme
Splash cognac
1/4 cup dry white wine
1/2 cup beef stock
1 cup black olives
1 cup green olives
1/2 pound shitake or chanterelle mushrooms,
    (sautéed in 2 tablespoon butter and seasoned with
    salt, pepper, and lemon juice)

Lightly dust quail with flour. In skillet, cook bacon until crisp. Brown quail on both sides in butter in batches. Add all quail to skillet and flame with cognac. Add juniper berries, thyme, wine, beef stock, and olives. Cover and simmer over medium heat for 15 minutes. Add mushrooms and crumbled bacon and serve immediately.

Serves 8-12

Meats

Mission Canyon Stroganoff

4-ounces sweet butter
1-1/2 pounds fillet of beef, sliced in thin strips
3 tablespoons onion, finely chopped
1 box of fresh mushrooms, cut in thin slivers
1-1/2 teaspoons salt
Dash of ground pepper
2 tablespoons flour
1/2 cup dry, good-quality sherry
1 cup sour cream
1 cup whipping cream
1/2 dozen chives, finely chopped
1-1/2 tablespoons horseradish
Fresh parsley for garnish
Dutch-style egg noodles, cooked, enough for 4 people

Heat butter in a large skillet. Add the beef, onion, mushrooms, salt, and pepper. Sauté 3 minutes over high heat. Turn heat down to medium flame. Add flour and blend well, sauté a little longer, 5 minutes or less. Mix together the sherry, cream, chives, horseradish, and sour cream. Slowly add the meat mixture to the pan, bring to a boil and remove from heat immediately. Serve hot cooked noodles with fresh parsley as garnish.

Serves 4

Boeuf en Croute avec
Pâté Sauce Maderia

1/4 cup butter
1/3 cup each celery, onion, and parsley, coarsely chopped
1 package frozen Pepperidge Farm puffed pastry shells,
   or make fresh
Bay leaf
1 ounce cognac
1/4 cup madeira
Pinch rosemary
1 cup canned bouillon
2/3 cup pâté de foie gras (liver pâté)
1 whole tenderloin of beef, all fat and tendinous material
   removed: This should be the largest possible since you
   want a 3/4 inch slice for each person.

Smear the fillet generously with butter and sprinkle with salt and pepper. Put it in a flat pan with the celery, onion, and parsley, one bay leaf and a pinch of rosemary and roast it in a very hot oven (450°) for about 25 minutes. Remove from oven and let cool. While the pan is hot, add 1 ounce cognac; stir well to lift pan drippings. Stir in 1 cup beef bouillon, 1/3 cup pâté de foie gras, 1/4 cup Madeira. The sauce should be simmered for 15 minutes and strained. Plan to reheat it and serve it separately. The puff pastry will need to thaw out for about 40 minutes before it is rolled. Spread the remaining pâté around the fillet. Roll out the pastry in a rectangle about 1/8 inch thick, enclose the fillet and trim the edges of the pastry and press firmly together. Reroll leftover pastry and cut leaves or other decorations for the top. For a shiny crust, brush the surface with beaten egg yolks before baking. Bake the fillet on a baking sheet for about 20 minutes at 450° or until golden brown.

Serves 8

Burgundy Ribs

    2 2-1/2 pounds short ribs
    1 tablespoon salt
Sauce
    1/2 cup Burgundy
    1/3 cup red wine vinegar
    1 8-ounce can tomato sauce
    2 tablespoons tomato paste
    2 tablespoons oil
    2 tablespoons honey
    1 tablespoon Worcestershire sauce
    1 tablespoon prepared mustard
    1 clove garlic, minced
    1 teaspoon chili powder

Place ribs in large kettle with water to cover and salt. Bring to boil, cover, and simmer 1/2 hour. Combine wine, vinegar, tomato sauce, tomato paste, oil, honey, Worcestershire, mustard, garlic, and chili powder and simmer 10-15 minutes. Drain ribs and place in shallow pan. Brush with sauce and bake at 350° for 15-20 minutes or until tender.

Serves 4

T-Bone Steaks
with Mustard-Tarragon Butter

6 T-bone steaks 1-1/2 inches thick
Olive oil
6 cloves garlic, minced
8-ounces sweet butter, softened
1/4 cup dry mustard
1 tablespoon dry tarragon or 2 tablespoons fresh

Slash fat on steaks so that they will not curl up when grilled. Rub steaks with olive oil and one minced clove garlic per steak. Heat grill, brush with oil; cook steaks on one side 2-3 minutes to sear then turn. Continue to cook and turn and move steaks around grill for 8-10 minutes for medium rare. Mix butter, dry mustard, and tarragon. Serve steaks with a dollop of mustard-tarragon butter.

Serves 6

Fillet Steak Washington

2　pounds beef tenderloin, cut into 4 steaks (trimmed)
4　teaspoons clarified butter
Black peppercorns, coarsely ground
Salt, freshly ground
4　large mushrooms
1　pound puff pastry
1　teaspoon lemon juice
Cayenne
1　egg
15　cups corn oil

Roll out puff pastry. Take a cup or bowl that just fits over steak and use this to mark out a circle on your pastry. Repeat four times, cutting pastry about 1/2 inch wider than cup measurement. Take a saucer and cut rounds a good 1-inch wider than the size previously cut out. Repeat four times. Beat egg, squeeze lemon juice, peel mushrooms, and remove stalks.

Heat fry pan, season steaks with ground peppercorns, add clarified butter to pan. When hot sear steaks on both sides and around edges (4 minutes for well done each side, 2 minutes for rare). Remove steaks and cool. Place mushrooms into pan (vein side uppermost). Season with lemon juice, salt, and cayenne pepper. Turn mushrooms to cook till just darkened on seasoned side. Remove mushrooms and place on top of cooled steaks. Dry with cloth. Put small round of pastry on a board and brush lightly with beaten egg. Place steak in center with a mushroom on top. Brush larger pastry round with egg. Place pastry (egg-brushed side down) on top of mushroom and steak. Press edges of pastry together and crimp with a fork to seal completely. Place in a paper bag (or aluminum foil) and refrigerate overnight. Remove from refrigerator 30 minutes before cooking. Heat oil in deep fryer to 400° and lower pastries into oil very gently with a slotted spoon. Fry for 7 minutes. Drain on absorbent paper. Serve accompanied by small minted potatoes.

Serves 4

A special hint: The secret is to dry steak and mushrooms thoroughly before wrapping and storing in refrigerator.

Boeuf Bourguignon

3 pounds beef sirloin, cut into 1-inch cubes
4 tablespoons butter
2-1/2 tablespoons flour
2 tablespoons brandy
12 small white onions
1/2 pound fresh mushrooms, sliced
Thyme to taste
3/4 pound diced bacon
1 carrot, diced
2 tablespoons tomato paste
1-1/2 cup Burgundy
3/4 cup red port
3/4 cup dry sherry
1 10-ounce can beef bouillon
Pepper to taste
1 bay leaf
1 garlic clove
Cornstarch to thicken

Slice bacon and fry to a crisp golden brown. Shake beef cubes in flour and fry in the bacon drippings until browned. Fry small peeled onions in drippings until browned. Heat brandy in a small pan. Ignite and pour over browned beef. Add everything else, blending well. Bring to a boil. Turn down heat and let simmer for about 3 hours to blend flavors. Cover and refrigerate overnight. Heat and serve over rice.

This recipe doubles and triples easily . . . depending on your needs.

Serves 6

Grilled Bleu Cheese Beef Tenderloins

4 8-ounce beef tenderloin fillet steaks,
    cut at least 1-inch thick
1 clove garlic, cut in half
Salt
2 tablespoons cream cheese
4 tablespoons onion, finely chopped
4 tablespoons bleu cheese
Dash white pepper
Chopped parsley

Rub each steak with garlic half. Sprinkle with salt. Combine cream cheese, onion, bleu cheese, and pepper. Grill steaks 5-7 minutes per side. Top with cheese mixture and sprinkle with parsley.

Serves 4

Moussaka

2 long thin eggplants
Olive oil
Salt to taste

Meat Sauce

2 pounds ground round steak
2 medium onions, chopped
1/4 pound mushrooms, chopped
1/4 cup parsley, chopped
1 15-ounce can tomato sauce
Salt to taste
1/2 cup red wine
1/4 tablespoons cinnamon
1 garlic clove, crushed
1 teaspoon oregano
3 tablespoons bread crumbs to bind

Cheese Sauce

6 tablespoons butter
6 tablespoons flour
2 cups warm milk
4 egg yolks
6 ounces feta cheese
3/4 cup Parmesan cheese
1/8 teaspoon nutmeg
1/3 cup pine nuts

Peel and cut eggplant into 1-inch slices. Brush both sides with oil and season with salt. Place on cookie sheet and bake in 450° oven for 10 minutes on each side. Set aside. Brown meat and onions in oil. Add mushrooms, parsley, tomato sauce, salt, wine, cinnamon, garlic, and oregano. Blend in bread crumbs to bind. Set aside. Melt butter over medium heat, add flour until bubbly, then add warm milk. Stir until thickened to make white sauce. Beat egg yolks and add a few tablespoons of white sauce to yolks. Add eggs to white sauce with parsley, feta, and Parmesan. Layer in a casserole starting with eight slices eggplant, 1/3 meat sauce and 1/3 cheese sauce. Layer again and add pine nuts. Bake in 375° oven uncovered for 35-40 minutes. Cool slightly and slice.

Serves 6-8

Fillet in Madeira Sauce

4 pounds center cut fillet of beef, tied in 2 or 3 places
Salt and pepper
1/4 cup butter
1/2 cup Madeira
2 cups brown stock
Brown Stock
1 carrot, sliced
1 onion, chopped
1 stalk celery, chopped
3 tablespoons butter
3 cups beef stock
1/2 bay leaf
Pinch thyme
Sprig parsley
Garlic clove, minced
Salt and pepper to taste
1/4 cup butter

Combine all ingredients for brown stock and simmer, partially covered for 1 hour. When sauce is done, strain. Sprinkle fillet with salt and pepper and brown on all sides in a heavy skillet in 1/4 cup butter over moderately high heat. Roast fillet in preheated 450° oven basting it with butter every 5 minutes for 20-25 minutes. Transfer to a cutting board and let cool for 10 minutes. Pour fat from pan and add Madeira; stir over moderately high heat, scraping up the brown bits from bottom and sides of pan. Add 2 cups brown stock, bring to boil and cook over moderately high heat for 5 minutes or until it is reduced to 1-1/2 cups. Remove pan from heat and swirl 1/4 cup butter into Madeira sauce. Cut the fillet into 3/4 inch slices and spoon a little sauce over. Serve remaining sauce in a sauceboat.

Serves 6

Grilled Lamb with Herbs and Vinegar

3 to 4 pounds leg of lamb
3 cloves garlic, minced
3/4 cup olive oil
1/4 cup red wine vinegar
3/4 cup onion, chopped
2 teaspoons Dijon mustard
2 teaspoons salt
1/2 teaspoon oregano
1/2 teaspoon basil
1/4 teaspoons freshly ground pepper
1 bay leaf, crushed

Have the butcher butterfly the leg of lamb or do it yourself by carefully removing the bone (being careful not to pierce the outer skin), and spreading the meat flat, in effect doubling its width. Place lamb, fat side down, in a shallow pan. In bowl or blender, make a marinade by combining the remaining ingredients and blending well. Pour marinade over lamb, cover tightly, and refrigerate overnight, turning lamb at least once. Remove lamb from refrigerator 1 hour before cooking. Barbecue over hot coals for about 30 minutes for medium rare. Turn occasionally and baste with marinade every 10 minutes. Slice diagonally when serving.

Serves 4-6

Provincial Lamb Stew with Tomatoes, Olives, Rosemary, and Sage

4 pounds lamb shoulder, cut up for stew
2 carrots, sliced
2 onions, chopped
1/3 cup olive oil
1 tablespoon fresh rosemary
1/2 teaspoon dried rosemary
2 teaspoons sage
2 bay leaves
3 2-inch pieces orange rind
3 tablespoons olive oil
1 28-ounce can Italian-style tomatoes,
   drained and coarsely chopped
4 garlic cloves, minced
1 cup dry white wine
2 cups beef stock
2 dozen Greek-style olives, pitted and chopped

Place lamb in large bowl or enamelled pot along with carrots, onions, olive oil, rosemary, sage, bay leaves, and orange rind. Sprinkle with salt and pepper and marinate overnight. In a heavy skillet heat 3 tablespoons olive oil and brown lamb pieces. Remove lamb to a casserole, add marinade (remove orange rind), tomatoes, garlic, wine, and stock. Cover and simmer. Preheat oven to 350°. Place casserole in oven for 2-3 hours or until lamb is tender. Remove lamb from casserole, skim off fat and add chopped olives. Bring to a simmer on top of stove. Return lamb to casserole to heat through. Garnish with parsley and serve.

Serves 8

Vegetable Stuffed Leg of Lamb

1 5 pound leg of lamb, boned and butterflied
1 tablespoon fresh rosemary or 1 teaspoon dried
2 teaspoons garlic, minced
1/4 pound spinach leaves, stemmed
4 medium carrots, cooked
4 whole pimientos, drained
1/2 thin sliced onion
1/4 cup fresh parsley, minced
Salt
3/4 teaspoon pepper
1/4 teaspoon cayenne
2 medium celery stalks, chopped
2 medium carrots, chopped
1/4 cup dry vermouth
1 cup chicken stock

Preheat oven to 325°. Lay meat flat, fat side down with long edge toward you. Sprinkle with rosemary and garlic. Cover with spinach. Arrange the four cooked carrots across center of meat in two rows. Surround with pimientos. Scatter onion and sprinkle with parsley, salt, pepper, and cayenne. Start at short end and roll-up meat tightly. Tie at 2-inch intervals. Place on a rack in a roasting pan. To bottom of pan add chopped carrots and onion. Season. Insert meat thermometer and roast to 130° for medium rare—about 1-1/2 hours. Add up to 1/2 cup water to pan to keep vegetables from sticking. When meat is done, let sit 15-20 minutes. Meanwhile, pour off fat from pan. Stir in stock and mash vegetables in liquid. Boil, strain, season. Spoon sauce over meat.

Serves 6-8

Rosemary Skewered Lamb Chops

8 small loin lamb chops 1-1/2 inches thick
8 sprigs rosemary
1/2 cup olive oil
4 garlic cloves
Salt and pepper
Lemon wedges

Using a metal skewer, bore a hole through the tail of the lamb chop to the center of the chop. Insert rosemary sprig with tufted end exposed. Rub each chop with olive oil and garlic. Grill for total time of 10 minutes, turning frequently. Serve with lemon wedges.

Serves 4

Filet d'Agneau—Sauce de Champignons

4 racks of lamb, boned, about 9 chops to a rack
Bones from the lamb
2 onions
4 cloves garlic
1 teaspoon thyme
4 ounces dried imported mushrooms
   (Porcini, Chanterelles, Morels)
1/2 pound fresh mushrooms, cut off stem ends
4 tablespoons butter
3 shallots
2 cups heavy cream
2 tablespoons lemon juice, or to taste
4 tablespoons reserved juices from bones
Reserved mushroom liquid
Madeira (about 1/4 cup or less)
Ask the butcher to bone the racks of lamb and chop the bones into 2-inch pieces.

Early in the day: Roast lamb bones with onions, garlic, and thyme in a preheated 425° oven for about 1 hour, or until brown. Remove bones and pour fat from pan, then add Madeira and stir over moderately high heat, scraping up the brown bits from the bottom and sides of pan. Strain reserve juices.

Sauce: Wash dried mushrooms in water to clean thoroughly. Drain. Pour over them boiling water to cover and soak at least 30 minutes. Strain liquid through a strainer lined with a double thickness of cheesecloth. Reduce liquid and reserve at least by half by boiling. Cut the reconstituted mushrooms into small pieces, discarding tough stems. Drop fresh mushrooms into boiling, salted water for a minute. Drain and discard water. Coarsely chop fresh mushrooms. Melt butter in skillet. Add finely minced shallots and cook about 5 minutes. Add all mushrooms and cream and simmer until reduced and thickened slightly. Stir in lemon juice, reserved juices from roasting pan and enough mushroom liquid to achieve a proper consistency. Taste for seasoning. Lace with Madeira and set aside until needed.

Serves 8

Lamb Chops à la Charles

16 lamb rib chops, with fat removed
3 slices Prosciutto, minced
1 large chicken breast, finely chopped
2 shallots, finely chopped
4 teaspoons butter
Pinch thyme, salt, pepper
1/2 teaspoon dried tarragon leaves
Ground black pepper
1 cup dry white wine
4 large mushrooms, chopped
Fila dough or puff pastry

Season lamb chops and broil to medium rare on both sides. Drain and cool. Sauté Prosciutto, chicken, mushrooms and shallots in butter. Season with thyme, salt, and pepper. Cook for 5 minutes and remove to a plate. Simmer tarragon and pinch of ground pepper in 1/2 cup of wine until reduced. Add the chicken mixture and the other 1/2 cup of wine. Continue cooking over high heat for another 10 minutes. Spoon meat mixture onto each chop. Layer and butter three sheets of fila dough. Cut into four long strips. Repeat for sixteen strips. Wrap each strip around a chop. May be refrigerated at this point. Let stuffing mixture cool before wrapping. Bring to room temperature and then bake in 375° oven for 25-30 minutes.

Serves 6

NOTE: If you use frozen pastry dough, defrost and roll out dough until paper thin. Cut into pieces about 4-inch square and use to wrap chops.

Fennel Stuffed Pork Chops

6 pork chops, cut 1 inch thick
Salt and pepper to season
2 cups fine dry bread crumbs
1 cup apple, finely chopped
1/4 cup onion, finely chopped
2 tablespoons butter, melted
1/2 tablespoon fennel seed, crushed
1/4 tablespoon salt
2 tablespoons water
2 tablespoons oil

Cut pocket in each chop for stuffing. Season chops with a little salt and pepper. Combine crumbs, apple, onion, butter, fennel seed, and salt. Sprinkle with 2 tablespoons water and toss. Stuff mixture into pockets. In large skillet that can go into oven, brown chops slowly on both sides in hot oil, about 10-15 minutes. Drain excess fat. Bake, uncovered in 350° oven for 45 minutes or until meat is tender.

Serves 6

Best Oven Barbecued Ribs

1 rack of pork spareribs
1 large onion, grated
1 cup ketchup
1 cup water
1/2 cup brown sugar
1/2 cup vinegar
2 tablespoons Worcestershire sauce
1 tablespoon dry mustard
8 drops Tabasco sauce
1 tablespoon salt

Preheat oven to 350°. Trim excess fat off spareribs and slice rack of ribs into individual ribs. Broil fat off ribs and to seal in juice, about 5 minutes a side. Place broiled ribs in roasting pans. Grate onion and combine rest of ingredients together to make sauce. Pour over ribs and bake for 30 minutes. Remove to baste with more sauce. Return to oven and bake, removing to baste every 30 minutes, for a total of 2 hours cooking time. Sauce will thicken as it cooks. Note: Sauce is also great on chicken.

Serves 4-6

Roast Pork with Marjoram

1 **center-cut pork loin with bones, approximately 4 pounds**
1 **large clove garlic, peeled and cut lengthwise into 10 slivers**
Salt to taste
Freshly ground pepper to taste
1 **tablespoon olive oil**
1 **tablespoon dried marjoram**
2 **small onions, peeled and quartered**
1 **cup chicken broth**

Preheat the oven to 400°. Make 10 gashes in the fat and between the flesh and bone of the pork loin. Insert one sliver of garlic in each gash. Sprinkle the meat on all sides with salt and pepper. Rub the pork all over with olive oil and sprinkle with marjoram. Arrange the pork fat side up on a roasting pan and arrange onions around it. Place in the oven and bake 30 minutes. Turn the roast fat side down and continue baking 30 minutes, basting occasionally. Turn the pork fat side up and continue baking for another 30 minutes, basting occasionally. Remove the pork and pour off the fat from the pan. Add the broth and return the pork fat side down to the pan. Return to the oven and continue baking, basting often, about 30 minutes longer. Discard the onions. Carve the meat and serve it with the pan liquid.

Serves 4-6

Pork Tenderloin Javanese

2 pounds pork tenderloin
6 Brazil nuts, chopped
1 cup onion, minced
2 cloves garlic, minced
1/4 cup lemon juice
1/4 cup soy sauce
2 tablespoons brown sugar
2 tablespoons ground coriander
1/4 teaspoon red pepper, crushed
1/4 cup olive or vegetable oil

Trim excess fat from meat. Cut meat into 1-inch cubes. Combine nuts, onion, garlic, lemon juice, soy sauce, sugar, seasonings, and oil. Add pork cubes, marinate for 6-8 hours in refrigerator. Place pork on skewers, reserve marinade. Grill over coals, or broil for about 10 minutes on each side, brushing once on each side with the reserved marinade. Serve with hot rice.

Serves 4

Pork Tenderloin Kobe Style

2 1-1/2 pound pork tenderloins
1/2 cup soy sauce
1 3-inch piece ginger root, mashed
Grated peel and juice of 1 orange
2 garlic cloves, minced
1/4 cup honey
1/4 cup sesame seeds
Orange segments

Mirin Sauce
1/2 cup Mirin (sweet sake)
1/2 cup soy sauce
1/2 cup chicken stock
1 1-inch piece ginger root, sliced thinly
1 clove garlic
Juice of 1 orange
1 tablespoon cornstarch
Water

Place pork in shallow pan. Combine soy sauce, ginger, orange peel and juice, and garlic in small bowl. Marinate at least 3 hours. Remove from marinade, roll in honey and sprinkle with sesame seeds. Place on rack in roasting pan and roast at 475° about 30 minutes. Slice and garnish with orange segments. Serve with sauce.

Combine Mirin, soy sauce, chicken stock, ginger, garlic, and orange juice in sauce pan. Mix cornstarch with enough water to make a thin paste, stir into mixture. Bring to simmer and cook until sauce thickens.

Serves 4-6

French Canadian Tourtière

Pastry for 2 crusts
1 pound ground pork
1 pound ground beef
1 medium onion, ground or finely chopped
1/2 teaspoon allspice
1/2 teaspoon cloves
1 teaspoon salt
1/2 teaspoon pepper
2 teaspoon savory
1 teaspoon cinnamon
1/2 teaspoon nutmeg
1/4 teaspoon celery pepper
2 cloves garlic, crushed
1 cup water
3/4 to 1 cup bread crumbs (or 2 medium potatoes
    cooked and mashed)

Roll pastry, line a 9-inch pie plate with one pastry crust. Set aside. Put next thirteen ingredients into extra large sauce pan. Bring to boil, simmer 20 minutes. Stir occasionally. Remove from heat. Slowly add crumbs and stir. Mixture should be moist and thick. Cool. Pour mixture into pastry shell. Dampen outer edge with water. Cover with second pastry crust. Press edges to seal. Cut several slits in top crust. Bake in 375 oven for 45 minutes or until browned. Cut into wedges to serve. Serve hot.

Serves 8

Veal Chops in Brandy Cream Sauce

2 tablespoons green onion, chopped
2 tablespoons butter or margarine
1 tablespoon all-purpose flour
1/2 teaspoon dried marjoram leaves
1/4 teaspoon instant chicken bouillon powder
1/4 teaspoon white pepper
1 cup whipping cream
1-1/2 teaspoons dried parsley flakes
    (or 1 tablespoon snipped fresh parsley)
1 tablespoon brandy
1 tablespoon Madeira wine
1 teaspoon sugar
2 tablespoons butter or margarine
4 1-inch thick veal chops

For sauce, in medium sauce pan on medium-high heat sauté green onion in butter until tender-crisp. Blend in flour, marjoram, bouillon powder, and pepper. Add sugar. Stir in cream. Add parsley. Cook, stirring constantly, until bubbly and thickened. Remove from heat. Stir in brandy and wine. Set aside. In medium skillet brown veal chops on both sides in butter. Cook in frying pan 3 or 4 minutes for medium rare. Reheat sauce. Serve over chops. Sprinkle with cayenne pepper.

Serves 4

Osso Buco with Gremolata

2 tablespoons unsalted butter

2 tablespoons olive oil

5 pounds veal shanks, cut into 2-inch pieces and tied with string around their circumference

1 cup all-purpose flour

2 medium onions, coarsely chopped

1 medium celery rib, coarsely chopped

3 garlic cloves, crushed

1 28-ounce can Italian peeled tomatoes, drained and coarsely chopped

2-1/2 tablespoons tomato paste

2 cups dry white wine or dry vermouth

1 cup chicken stock or canned broth

3 strips of lemon zest, about 2 inches long

4 sprigs parsley

1 large bay leaf

1/2 teaspoon marjoram

1/2 teaspoon basil

1/2 teaspoon thyme

Gremolata

1/2 cup minced parsley

Juice of 1 orange

1 tablespoon cornstarch

Water

3 medium garlic cloves, minced

1 tablespoon grated lemon zest

In a large flameproof casserole, melt the butter in the oil over moderate heat. Dredge the veal in the flour and shake off any excess. Working in batches, sauté the veal on all sides until golden brown. Do not crowd the pan. Remove to a bowl. Add the onions, carrot, celery, and garlic to casserole. Cover and cook until the vegetables are tender, about 15 minutes. Add tomatoes, tomato paste, chicken stock, lemon zest, parsley, and herbs. Cook for 15 minutes. Transfer sauce to sauce pan. Return veal to casserole. Add the wine or vermouth. Cook over moderately high heat until wine has evaporated. Add sauce and simmer for 1 hour. Remove veal from casserole and keep warm. Increase heat to high and boil, stirring frequently until sauce thickens. Pour over meat. Mix gremolata ingredients and sprinkle on top of sauce when served.

Serves 8

Veal Pizzaiola

2 thin slices of veal (leg cut)
Freshly ground salt
Freshly ground black pepper
4 tablespoons olive oil
3 cloves garlic
1-1/2 pounds tomatoes
2 thin slices Mozzarella cheese
Sprig oregano (or 1/2 teaspoon dried)
Worcestershire sauce
1 tablespoon parsley
Parmesan cheese
2 teaspoons Worcestershire sauce

Pound veal slices until very thin and remove sinew from side of meat. Smash and finely chop garlic. Skin tomatoes and chop roughly. Finely slice Mozzarella cheese. Finely chop parsley. Place 2 tablespoons olive oil into a heated fry pan, add veal slices seasoned with salt and pepper, lower heat under pan and lightly fry veal on both sides. Place 2 tablespoons olive oil into a separate pan on heat and fry garlic gently. Add tomatoes and oregano. Season with salt and pepper. Reduce heat and cook slowly a few minutes. Add meat juices from fry pan to tomatoes. Reserve. Place a slice of Mozzarella cheese on each veal slice and using a slotted spoon put tomato pulp and some of sauce over veal. Cover and allow to simmer for 5 minutes. Press remaining sauce through a sieve and add parsley. Place veal and tomatoes on a serving dish, powder heavily with Parmesan cheese and brown under broiler for 2 minutes. Serve sauce separately in a sauceboat.

Serves 2

Butterflied Veal Chops with Arugula

6 1/2 pound rib veal chops about 3/4 inch thick
6 garlic cloves, minced
2 cups dry white wine
1-1/2 teaspoons salt
4 cups loosely packed arugula leaves, coarsely chopped
   (about 2 bunches)
2 tablespoons olive oil
1 teaspoon red wine vinegar
Freshly ground pepper

Spread chops with garlic. Mix wine and salt and marinate chops at room temperature 2 hours. Mix arugula with oil, vinegar, and pepper. Grill chops serve with arugula artfully arranged.

Serves 6

Mixed Grill—Sweetbreads, Game Hens, and Hot Sausage

1 to 1-1/2 pounds sweetbreads
3 fresh Cornish games hens
6 hot Italian sausages
Rosemary
1 clove garlic
Juice of 1 lemon
1/4 cup melted butter
1/4 cup olive oil
1/2 cup beer
Salt and pepper to taste

Soak sweetbreads in cold water 30 minutes. Change water in pan and bring to simmer for 2-3 minutes. Drain and reserve. Slit the game hens in half and remove backbone. Rub hens with rosemary, garlic, and lemon. Mix together in pot over medium heat, butter, beer, and oil. Lightly oil grill. Sweetbreads will take 25 minutes to cook, hens 20 minutes, and sausages 15 minutes. Baste sweetbreads with butter-beer mixture and grill. Grill game hens and sausages. Baste and season with salt and pepper.

Serves 6

Orange-Lemon Glaze

1/2 cup water
1/2 cup orange juice
1/3 cup soy sauce
1 tablespoon cornstarch
1 tablespoon onion, minced
1 tablespoon lemon rind, grated
1 tablespoon ginger root, grated
2 cloves garlic, mashed to a paste
1/2 tablespoon salt
1/4 tablespoon pepper

Combine all ingredients in saucepan and bring to a boil, simmering for 3 minutes or until sauce thickens. Use glaze to coat ribs, chicken or chops during last minutes of grilling.

Yield 1-1/2 cups

Lamb Marinade

Curry powder
Oregano
Garlic (fresh and powder)
Chablis to marinate

Combine all ingredients with water to form a paste. Rub all over lamb. Marinate for 24 hours in Chablis. Barbecue or roast in oven.

Flank Steak Marinade

1/2 cup soy sauce
1/4 cup wine (whatever is handy)
5 tablespoons honey
1 small onion, chopped
2 tablespoons parsley, chopped

Mix all ingredients and pour over flank steak (no metal or aluminum containers—use plastic or glass). Marinate all day, turning frequently. Remove steak from marinade and barbecue or broil 5 minutes per side. Cut in 1 inch strips across the grain to serve.

Barbecue Sauce California Style

1/3 cup cider vinegar
1/4 cup chili sauce
1 8-ounces can tomato sauce
1/4 cup onion, chopped
2 tablespoons brown sugar
1 tablespoon Worcestershire sauce
1 tablespoon dry mustard

In medium saucepan combine all ingredients. Bring to a boil, reduce heat, simmer uncovered 30 minutes. Serve on chicken, spareribs, hamburger, steak.

Yield 1-1/2 cups

Barbecue Sauce Texas Style

1/2 cup light beer
1-1/2 cups chili sauce
2 tablespoons onion, grated
2 tablespoons vinegar
2 tablespoons sugar
2 tablespoons Worcestershire sauce
1 tablespoons chili powder
1 bay leaf

In medium saucepan combine all ingredients with 1/2 cup water, mix well. Bring to a boil, reduce heat and simmer, covered, stirring occasionally for 3 minutes.

To be used with beef, spareribs, hamburgers.

Yield 2-1/3 cups

Mustard Seed and
Black Peppercorn Marinade

2 tablespoons mustard seed
2 tablespoons crushed peppercorns
1 tablespoon Dijon mustard
1 clove garlic, minced
4 tablespoons port to marinate

Combine all ingredients. Press mixture onto both sides of meat. Marinate in port at room temperature for at least 2 hours or overnight before grilling.

Bed and Breakfast

Zucchini-Basil Muffins

2 **eggs**
3/4 **cup milk**
2/3 **cup oil**
2 **cups flour**
1/4 **cup sugar**
1 **tablespoon baking powder**
1 **teaspoon salt**
2 **cups shredded zucchini, coarsely shredded**
2 **tablespoons fresh basil, minced**
1/4 **cup grated fresh Parmesan cheese**

Beat eggs, stir in milk and oil. Combine flour, sugar, baking powder, and salt. Mix until just moistened but not completely blended. Stir in zucchini and basil. Fill oiled muffin cups to 3/4 full and sprinkle tops with Parmesan cheese. Bake at 425° approximately 20 minutes.

Yield 10-18 muffins

Sour Cream Peach Muffins
with Honey Butter

Muffins
- 1 cup chopped peaches (fresh or canned)
- 1 cup sour cream
- 1 egg
- 1/4 cup melted butter
- 2 cups flour
- 1 tablespoon baking powder
- 1/4 teaspoon baking soda
- 1/4 teaspoon salt
- 1/4-1/2 cup sugar

Honey butter
- 1/2 cup butter
- 1/3 cup of honey
- Blend and mix together thoroughly

Preheat oven to 370°. Grease pans or use paper liners. Blend together peaches, sour cream, and egg. Stir in butter. Mix flour, baking powder, baking soda, salt, and sugar. Pour sour cream, peach mixture over flour mixture and stir only to blend. Put in muffin pans and bake for 35 minutes.

Serve with honey butter

Yield 1 dozen

Apple Fritters

1-1/2 cups flour
1-1/2 teaspoons baking powder
1/4 teaspoon salt
2 eggs
2/3 cup milk
4 apples
Vegetable oil to cover bottom of frying pan
1/2 cup sugar

Combine flour, baking powder, and salt. Beat eggs with milk and add sugar. Combine flour and egg mixtures. Core and slice apples with food processor blade—the thinner the slices, the faster they cook. It is not necessary to remove skin.

Add apples to batter and gently fold until apples are coated with batter. Using a large spoon, drop batter into hot oil in frying pan. Flatten slightly. Cook until golden brown, turning once. Serve hot with powdered sugar or syrup.

May be kept warm in the oven until ready to serve. Lay on paper towels to absorb any extra oil.

Serves 4-6

St. Barbara's Bread

1/4 cup milk
1/4 cup sugar
2 teaspoons unsalted butter
1/4 teaspoon salt
1/2 teaspoon active dry yeast
2 teaspoons warm water (105°-115°)
1 egg
1/2 teaspoon lemon juice
1/2 teaspoon nutmeg
1/2 teaspoon allspice
1/2 teaspoon cinnamon
1 to 1-1/2 cups flour
1/3 cup slivered almonds
Confectioners' Icing:
    Mix the following ingredients thoroughly:
    1/2 cup sifted confectioners' sugar
    1/2 teaspoon vanilla
    1-2 tablespoons milk

Heat milk, sugar, salt, and butter to warm 105-115°. Dissolve yeast in warm water of the same temperature. Set aside 5 minutes.

Combine yeast mixture, milk mixture, egg, lemon juice, nutmeg, allspice, and cinnamon. Add 1 cup flour and sliced almonds. Mix thoroughly. Add enough remaining flour to make soft dough. Knead on lightly floured surface until smooth, 10 minutes.

Place in greased bowl, turning to coat top. Cover and let rise in warm place until doubled, about 1 hour. Punch down dough and divide into thirds. Make three ropes and braid. Place on greased baking sheet.

Let rise until doubled, about 30 minutes. Bake 350° 34-40 minutes. Cool. Frost by drizzling icing back and forth. Decorate with whole almonds, if desired.

Yield 1 loaf

Pineapple Nut Bread

3/4 cup brown sugar
1/3 cup butter
2 large eggs
1 8-ounce can sweetened crushed pineapple, undrained
1 teaspoon vanilla extract
1 cup nuts, chopped
2-1/4 cups sifted flour
2 teaspoons baking powder
1/4 teaspoon baking soda
1/4 teaspoon salt
Topping
1 tablespoon sugar
1/4 teaspoon cinnamon
1/4 cup chopped nuts

Preheat oven to 350°. Cream butter and sugar. Add eggs and beat just enough to blend. Stir in the entire contents of the pineapple can, the vanilla, and the nuts. Sift together the flour, baking powder, baking soda, and salt. Stir the dry ingredients into the pineapple mixture just until there are no more dry lumps; do not overmix. Turn into a buttered loaf pan and set aside for 15 minutes. Combine the ingredients for the topping and sprinkle over the batter, pressing in lightly with the back of a spoon. Bake for 1 hour or until bread tests done.

Yield 1 loaf

Lemon Poppy Seed Tea Cakes

2/3 cup cake flour
1/4 teaspoon baking soda
1/4 cup butter, softened
2/3 cup sugar, divided
2 eggs, separated
1-1/2 tablespoons lemon juice
1 teaspoon vanilla
1-1/2 teaspoons lemon rind, grated
2-1/2 tablespoons poppy seeds
1/4 cups sour cream
Powdered sugar

Preheat oven to 375°. Butter and flour six muffin cups. Sift flour and baking soda into a small bowl. Cream butter and sugar in a large bowl. Slowly add 1/3 cup sugar and beat until fluffy. Beat in egg yolks one at a time, then beat in lemon juice, vanilla, lemon rind, and poppy seeds. Add flour mixture and sour cream alternately to the batter and combine well. In a large bowl beat the egg whites to soft peaks. Gradually add 1/3 cups sugar and continue beating until stiff peaks form. Stir 1/4 of meringue into batter to lighten it, then fold in the remaining meringue gently but thoroughly. Divide the batter among the muffin cups. Bake 20-25 minutes, or until golden. Turn onto a rack and sift powdered sugar over tops.

Yield 6 muffins

Avocado Bread

1-1/2 cups sugar
2 eggs
1/2 cup butter or margarine, softened
1 cup avocado, mashed
1/2 cup sour milk or buttermilk
1-1/2 cups flour
1/2 teaspoon cinnamon
1/2 teaspoon allspice
1/2 teaspoon nutmeg
1/2 teaspoon salt
1 teaspoon baking soda
1/2 cup chopped dates
1/2 cup chopped walnuts
1/2 cup raisins

Mix together sugar, eggs, butter, or margarine, avocado, and milk. Set aside. In another bowl mix together flour, spices, salt, soda, date, walnuts, and raisins. Stir this mixture into the liquid mixture. The batter will be very stiff. Bake in two greased loaf pans for 1 hour or until done at 300°. Remove from pan and cool on racks. This bread freezes very well.

Yield 2 loaves

Stollen

4 cups flour, sifted
1 tablespoon baking powder
3 eggs, beaten to blend
1 cup sugar
1 teaspoon vanilla extract
1/2 teaspoon almond extract
1 teaspoon rum extract
1/4 teaspoon cardamom
1/4 teaspoon nutmeg
1/2 cup butter
1/4 cup solid shortening
1/2 pound farmers' cheese
2/3 cup currants
1-1/2 cups raisins
1/4 pound hazelnuts, ground
1/4 pound candied lemon peel, finely chopped
Powdered sugar

Preheat oven to 350°. Mix flour and baking powder on a wooden board and make a well in the middle. Put eggs, sugar, vanilla, almond and rum extracts, cardamom, and nutmeg into well and mix thoroughly, adding some of the flour until a thick paste forms. Add butter, shortening, farmers' cheese, currants, raisins, hazelnuts, and lemon peel, and cover the entire mixture with flour. Combine all ingredients well and form dough into an oval-shaped loaf about 1 inch long. Place the loaf on a buttered and floured baking sheet and bake for 1 hour. Cool on a rack. Just before serving, sift powdered sugar over the loaf.

Yield 1 loaf

Cranberry Pecan Holiday Bread

2 cups all purpose flour
2 teaspoons baking powder
1/4 cup cold butter, cut into pieces
1 cup sugar
1/2 cup pecans, chopped
2 teaspoons grated orange zest
1 egg
2/3 cup orange juice, preferably fresh
2 cups fresh, whole cranberries
1 tablespoon milk

Preheat the oven to 350°. Grease a 9 x 5-inch loaf pan.

In a large bowl, mix together the flour and baking soda. Cut in the butter until the mixture resembles fine bread crumbs. Add the sugar, the pecans, and the orange zest and toss to blend.

In another bowl, beat the egg until frothy and add the orange juice until blended. Pour this over the dry ingredients and mix gently. Before all the flour is mixed in, add the cranberries and stir thoroughly.

Put the batter into the prepared pan and smooth evenly with a spatula. Brush the milk over the top of the batter and sprinkle 1 teaspoon of sugar over the batter.

Bake for 1 hour and 15 minutes of until the loaf is golden brown and crusty and a tester inserted in the center of the loaf comes out clean. Cool for 20 minutes and then remove from the pan and place on a rack to cool further. This bread is best made ahead of time and can be eaten cold or reheated or toasted. It is tart and delicious.

Yield 1 loaf

Sour Cream Coffee Cake

Topping
- 1 cup pecans or walnuts
- 1/4 cup melted butter
- 1/4 cup white sugar
- 1/3 cup brown sugar
- 1 teaspoon cinnamon

Chop nuts in processor and put in small bowl. Combine remaining ingredients and mix with nuts. Set aside.

Cake
- 2 cups sifted flour
- 1 teaspoon baking powder
- 1 teaspoon baking soda
- 1/2 teaspoon salt
- 1/2 cup butter
- 1 teaspoon vanilla extract
- 2 eggs
- 1 cup sour cream
- 1 cup sugar

Preheat oven to 350°. Butter a 9" springform pan. Sift together flour, baking powder, baking soda, and salt. Set aside. Put butter, sugar, vanilla, and eggs in food processor. Mix until smooth. Repeat with remaining flour and sour cream and process until smooth. Repeat with remaining flour and sour cream. Scrape down sides thoroughly. Spread half the batter in springform pan. Evenly sprinkle half the topping over the batter. Cover with remaining batter and topping. Bake 50 minutes or until done. Cool for 10 minutes before removing from pan.

Serves 8-12

Pear and Apple Coffee Cake

1/2 cup softened butter or margarine
1 cup granulated sugar
2 eggs
1 teaspoon vanilla
2 cups all-purpose flour
1 teaspoon baking soda
1 teaspoon baking powder
1/2 teaspoon salt
1 cup sour cream
2 cups finely chopped apples and pear (2 apples and 1 pear)
1 cup brown sugar
1/2 cup chopped walnuts or pecans
2 tablespoons butter or margarine, softened
1 teaspoon cinnamon

Grease 13 x 9 x 2-inch baking pan—preheat oven to 350°.

Cream butter and sugar together. Mix in eggs and vanilla. Beat well. Sift together flour, baking soda, baking powder, and salt. Stir flour mixture in alternately with sour cream. Fold in apple and pear chips. Spread butter in pan.

Mix brown sugar, chopped nuts, butter, and cinnamon. Sprinkle over batter. Bake until toothpick comes out clean. 45-55 minutes 350°.

Yield 1 loaf

Raspberry Riches

Cake
- 1 cup sifted all purpose flour
- 3/4 cup sugar
- 1/2 teaspoon baking powder
- 1/4 teaspoon baking soda
- 1/4 teaspoon salt
- 1 egg
- 1/3 cup buttermilk or whole milk
- 1/2 teaspoon vanilla extract
- 1/3 cup unsalted butter, melted and cooled to room temperature
- 1-1/4 cups fresh red raspberries

Sugar Crumb Topping
- 1/2 cup firmly packed light brown sugar
- 2 teaspoons flour
- 1 teaspoon unsalted butter, cut into small pieces
- 1-1/2 teaspoons (1/2 ounce) semi-sweet chocolate, grated

Preheat oven to 375°. Butter a 9-inch round glass baking pan. Sift together the flour, sugar, baking powder, baking soda, and salt into a large mixing bowl. In second bowl, beat together egg, milk, and vanilla until smooth. Stir in butter. Pour liquid mixture into flour mixture. Beat with a wooden spoon until smooth. Spread batter evenly in prepared pan. Sprinkle with fresh raspberries.

Prepare topping: With metal blade in processor, add all topping ingredients to bowl and process until like fine crumbs. Sprinkle over raspberries in pan. Bake until brown, about 40-45 minutes. Cool cake until warm and serve.

Serves 8-12

Wild Rice and Mushroom Pancakes with Smoked Salmon, Avocado, and Caviar

1 cup cooked wild rice, drained
2 tablespoons onion, chopped
4 tablespoons butter
1 cup flour
2 tablespoons baking powder
1 teaspoon salt
3 eggs, beaten
1-1/2 cups buttermilk
1/2 pound mushrooms, chopped
1/2-3/4 pound smoked salmon, thinly sliced
2-3 medium avocados, peeled and sliced
1 cup sour cream
1 small jar black caviar

Sauté onion and mushrooms until tender, but not browned. Remove from heat.

Beat eggs, stir in buttermilk and set aside. Blend flour, soda, and salt. Gradually add flour mixture to liquid. Add mushrooms, onions, and remaining butter. Stir until well blended. Add wild rice.

Spoon 1 tablespoon batter onto heated and buttered heavy skillet. Turn when bubbles appear. Remove to warm platter when cooked. Can be made ahead and reheated in foil.

Cover each pancake with salmon slices. Top with 1 tablespoon sour cream and garnish with avocado slice and caviar. Pancakes should be served warm.

Yield 2 dozen pancakes

Cottage Cheese Pancakes

3 eggs
1 cup cottage cheese
1/4 cup regular or whole wheat flour
1/4 teaspoon vanilla
1 teaspoon vanilla
2 tablespoons vegetable oil

Put eggs, oil, cottage cheese and vanilla in blender. Blend well. Add flour and blend briefly until incorporated throughout. Cook as for any pancake and serve topped with maple syrup, or honey, jam or powdered sugar.

Sour Cream Pancakes

2 eggs (beaten)
1/2 teaspoon baking soda
3 heaping teaspoons flour
1/4 teaspoon salt
1/2 pint sour cream

Beat all ingredients together and cook on a very hot griddle. Pancakes should be silver dollar size to cook best.

Gourmet French Toast

6 eggs
1/2 cup orange juice
1/3 cup Grand Marnier liqueur
1/2 cup half-and-half
1/4 teaspoon salt
1/2 teaspoon vanilla
Peel of 1 orange, grated
1 loaf of cinnamon bread
4 tablespoons butter
Topping
1 cup maple syrup
1 cup honey
2 teaspoons dark rum
Mix the above ingredients together and just before using heat until warm, stirring constantly.

The night before serving: Beat eggs in large bowl. Add orange juice, Grand Marnier, half-and-half, vanilla, salt, and orange peel. Mix well. Cut eight slices of bread, each 1-inch thick; dip in liquid mixture, turning to coat well. Pour remaining liquid over. Cover with plastic wrap and refrigerate overnight.

Melt 1 teaspoon butter in a large skillet. Add bread a few slices at a time and cook the next morning over medium heat until browned. Continue adding butter and cooking in batches. Keep warm in oven. Serve with butter and topping.

Serves 6

The Olive House Summer
Fresh Fruit Crêpes

Fresh fruit, melons, blueberries, pineapple, strawberries, kiwi, peaches, etc.
Cream Cheese Filling
> **8 ounces cream cheese, softened**
> **1/2 teaspoon lemon peel, grated**
> **2 teaspoons fresh orange juice**
> **Half-and-half**

Honey Yogurt Dressing
> **8 ounces vanilla yogurt**
> **1/4 cup honey**
> **Dash of cinnamon, nutmeg**
> **1/2 teaspoon vanilla**

Combine cream cheese, and orange juice with enough half-and-half to make a spreading consistency. Set aside. Mix together yogurt, cinnamon, nutmeg, and vanilla. To assemble, place one warm crêpe on a plate. Spread cream cheese filling on crepe, top with fresh mixed fruit of your choosing. Fold crêpe in half and drizzle honey yogurt dressing on top. Top with fresh whipped cream and granola or nuts.

Yield 8-12 crêpes

Finnish Pancakes with Raspberry Sauce

4 eggs
1/2 cup sugar
1 cup flour
1/2 cup butter
1/2 teaspoon salt
3 cups milk
1/2 cup sour cream
12 ounces frozen raspberries, thawed

Melt butter in 9 x 13-inch pan in 350° oven. Mix all other ingredients, except raspberries, in a bowl. Add to butter in pan, mix and bake 1 hour at 350°.

Purée raspberries. Serve with bowl of raspberries and powdered sugar on side.

Serves 8

Mediterranean Omelette

Sauce
- 1 tablespoon butter
- 1 tablespoon olive oil
- 2 tablespoons onion, finely chopped
- 2 tablespoons green pepper, chopped
- 1 small clove garlic, minced
- 1 cup tomato sauce
- 1 teaspoon Worcestershire sauce
- 1/2 teaspoon dried basil
- 1/2 teaspoon dried oregano
- 1/8 teaspoon pepper

In a small saucepan melt butter and olive oil. Sauté onion, bell pepper, and garlic until soft but not browned. Stir in other ingredients and simmer, covered, 10 minutes.

Omelette
- 2 tablespoons butter
- 1/2 cup fresh mushrooms, sliced
- 8 eggs
- 1/4 cup milk
- 4 slices bacon, cooked crisp and crumbled
- 2 tablespoons green onion, chopped
- 1/4 teaspoon salt
- Dash pepper
- 1/2 cup sharp Cheddar cheese, shredded

Melt butter in 12-inch skillet. Sauté mushrooms until tender. Beat eggs with milk, bacon, green onion, salt, and pepper. Stir in mushrooms, then pour into skillet and cook over low heat until set, lifting edges of omelette to allow uncooked egg to cook. When egg is set, remove omelette from heat, sprinkle cheese over half, and fold in half onto platter. top with sauce and serve.

Serves 4

Chicken Omelette

4 egg yolks
Dash white pepper
4 egg whites
1/4 cup water
1/4 teaspoon salt
1/4 teaspoon cream of tartar
Butter or margarine
1 teaspoon flour
1/2 teaspoon chicken stock base
1/4 teaspoon celery salt
1 cup milk
3/4 cup cooked chicken, cubed
1 cup red grapes, seeded and quartered
1-1/4 cups Swiss cheese, grated
1/4 cup sliced almonds, toasted

In a small mixing bowl, beat egg yolks and pepper until thick and lemon-colored. In a small mixing bowl, beat egg whites, water, salt, and cream of tartar until stiff but not dry. Fold beaten yolks into whites. Melt 2 teaspoons butter in a 10-inch skillet with heatproof handle until just hot enough to sizzle a drop of water. Turn egg mixture into skillet. Cook over low heat on top of range until puffy and browned on bottom, about 5 minutes. Transfer to oven and bake at 325° 12-15 minutes or until knife inserted near center comes out clean.

To prepare sauce, melt 1 teaspoon butter. Blend in flour, chicken stock base, and celery salt. Cook over low heat until mixture is smooth. Remove from heat. Stir in milk. Heat to boiling, stirring constantly. Boil and stir 1 additional minute. Remove from heat and stir in chicken and grapes. Keep warm for serving.

To serve, remove omelette to heated platter. Score down the center with a sharp knife. Spread 1 cup of cheese and 1/2 cup of sauce over bottom half of omelette. Fold omelette in half and top with remaining 1/4 cup cheese. Spoon 1/2 cup sauce over omelette and pass remaining sauce when serving. Garnish with toasted almonds.

Serves 4

Santa Barbara Omelette

   2 eggs
   2 teaspoons water
   2 teaspoons butter
Filling
   1 tomato, diced
   1 scallion, sliced
   2 whole Ortega green chiles, cut into 8 slices
      or 2 tablespoons diced Ortega chiles
  1/2 cup grated Jack cheese
  1/2 cup grated Cheddar cheese
     Sliced avocado
     Green chile salsa
  1/4 teaspoon lemon pepper
     Dash of chervil

Melt the butter in pan over medium-low heat. Break the eggs in a bowl and add the water. Use a wire whisk to beat eggs 1-2 minutes. Pour eggs in pan. Allow to slightly harden on bottom. Using a spatula, push cooked part to middle of pan and allow liquid to run around edges. Continue to do this until eggs are set but not hard or brown. When eggs are firm, place filling across the top. Use spatula to fold omelette over the filling. Season with spices and cover and return to low heat for a few minutes to melt cheeses.

Serves 2

East Beach Brunch

12 slices white or wheat bread
2-3 tablespoons butter
6 tablespoons margarine
1/2 pound fresh mushrooms, sliced
2 cups onions, thinly sliced
Salt and pepper
1-1/2 pounds hot sausage
1 pound Cheddar cheese, grated
5 eggs
2-1/2 cups milk
1 teaspoon dry mustard
1 tablespoon Dijon mustard
1 teaspoon nutmeg
2 teaspoons salt
1/4 teaspoon pepper

Butter bread and cut into cubes. Sauté onions and mushroom in margarine until soft. Season and set aside. Crumble sausage and brown, then drain. Layer bread, onions and mushrooms, sausage, and cheese twice in a 9 x 13-inch casserole. Mix remaining ingredients and pour over all. Cover and refrigerate overnight. Preheat oven to 350° and bake uncovered for 1 hour.

Serves 9-12

Montecito Soufflé

8 slices day-old bread, cubed
2 cups milk
4 eggs, beaten to blend
8 ounces Cheddar cheese, shredded
1 small scallion, chopped (white and light green parts only)
1/2 teaspoon Worcestershire sauce
1/4 teaspoon pepper
1 teaspoon dry mustard
1 tablespoon brown sugar
1 cup small cooked shrimp

Butter a 1-quart soufflé dish. Combine all ingredients and pour into dish. Cover and refrigerate overnight. Preheat oven to 300° and bake, uncovered, for 1 hour, until puffed and light brown.

Serves 4-6

Soufflé au Fromage pour Deux

2 tablespoons butter
2 tablespoons flour
1/4 teaspoon dry mustard
1/4 teaspoon salt
Dash cayenne
1/2 cup milk
1 cup sharp Cheddar, grated
2 eggs
Variation
1/4 cup grated Parmesan
1/2 cup chopped cooked spinach, well drained

Melt butter, stir in flour and seasonings. Add milk all at once and cook over medium heat, stirring until thickened and bubbly. Remove from heat, add cheese, and stir until cheese melts. Thoroughly beat egg yolks, then slowly add cheese mixture, stirring constantly. Cool slightly. Beat egg whites to soft peaks. Stir a bit of the egg whites into the cheese mixture, then fold mixture into egg whites. Pour into ungreased 3-cup soufflé dish and bake in preheated 300° oven for 45-50 minutes. Serve with mushroom sauce.

Serves 2

Mushroom Sauce

1/2 cup fresh mushrooms, sliced
2 tablespoons scallions, finely chopped
2 tablespoons butter
1 tablespoon cornstarch
1/2 cup light cream
1/3 cup dry white wine
1/4 teaspoon salt
Pepper to taste

Combine cornstarch and cream; stir until cornstarch dissolves and set aside. In small saucepan, cook mushrooms and scallions in the butter until just tender. Add cream mixture to vegetables, stir in wine, parsley, and seasonings. Cook, stirring, until thick and bubbly.

Serves 2

Onion Quiche

Pastry
- 1-1/4 cups flour
- 1/2 teaspoon salt
- 6 tablespoons sweet butter, frozen
- 1 tablespoon Dijon mustard mixed
     with 2 tablespoons cold water

Filling
- 2 large onions
- 4 tablespoons butter
- Pinch of sugar
- 1/4 teaspoon salt
- Pepper
- Pinch of allspice
- Pinch of thyme
- 3 large eggs
- 1 cup heavy cream
- 2-3 tablespoons grated Gruyère cheese

Put flour in food processor with steel blade. Cut butter into small pieces and add along with salt. Process with on-off motion. Add mustard and water and turn on/off until dough begins to look damp and comes together.

Chill dough 30 minutes in refrigerator. Roll out dough on floured surface and put in quiche pan. Preheat oven to 400°. Place foil over pastry. Bake 10 minutes, remove foil. Cool.

Slice onions into thin rings and sauté 30 minutes in butter with sugar, salt, pepper, allspice, and thyme. Preheat oven to 375°.

Paint bottom of pre-baked pastry shell with Dijon mustard. Mix together eggs and cream and pour over onions. Sprinkle cheeses on top and bake about 30 minutes or until knife comes out clean.

Serves 6-8

Canyon Quiche

1 9-inch pastry shell, baked 5 minutes and cooled
6 slices bacon
3 eggs
1-1/2 cups half-and-half
1/2 teaspoon salt
1/2 teaspoon pepper
1/8 teaspoon nutmeg
2/3 cup Swiss cheese, grated
1/2 cup mushrooms, sliced
1/2 avocado, sliced

Preheat oven to 350°. Cook the bacon and drain. Crumble into pastry shell. Beat eggs, half-and-half, salt, pepper, and nutmeg. Pour over bacon in shell. Sprinkle the cheese evenly over the egg mixture, then add the mushrooms and avocado slices. Bake for 30 minutes. Serve hot or cold.

Serves 6-8

Tomato and Cheese Tart with Fresh Herbs

Crust

- 1-1/2 cups flour
- 1/4 teaspoon salt
- 6 tablespoons butter, frozen
- 1 egg
- 3 tablespoons sour cream

Place flour and salt in food processor and pulse 2-3 times to sift. Cut butter into twelve pieces and add to flour. Use quick on/off pulses to cut butter into flour until it resembles coarse meal. In a separate bowl, mix egg and sour cream. Add to dough in food processor and pulse until it forms a ball. Wrap and refrigerate for at least 1 hour or overnight. Roll out dough and place in 9-inch tart pan with removable bottom. Prick crust with a fork and chill 30 minutes. Preheat oven to 400° and bake crust 15 minutes or until golden brown. Allow to cool. Reduce oven heat to 375°.

Filling

- 4-5 medium ripe tomatoes, sliced 1/4 inch thick
- 1/4 teaspoon salt
- 1-1/2 tablespoons Dijon mustard
- 3/4 pound Swiss or Gruyère cheese, grated

Freshly ground pepper to taste

- 1 tablespoon mixed fresh herbs
  (basil, oregano, rosemary, thyme)
- 2 tablespoons Parmesan cheese, freshly grated
- 2 tablespoons olive oil

Place sliced tomatoes on a rack, sprinkle with salt, and let drain 10 minutes. Blot gently with a paper towel. Paint bottom of shell with mustard and scatter Swiss or Gruyère cheese evenly over bottom. Arrange tomato slices attractively on top of cheese. Season with pepper and Parmesan cheese. Mince herbs and sprinkle over tart. Drizzle olive oil over top of tart. Bake for 25 minutes, or until top is lightly browned.

Serves 6-8

Chile Relleno Casserole

14 ounce canned whole Ortega chiles
1/2 pound Cheddar cheese, grated
1/2 pound Monterey Jack cheese, grated
1/4 pound sliced ham or Turkey (optional)
2 eggs, separated
8 ounces evaporated milk
1-1/2 tablespoons flour
1 cup prepared salsa

Preheat oven to 325°. Slice open chiles, remove seeds, rinse and pat dry. Place half the chiles flat to cover the bottom of a 8 x 8-inch baking dish. Cover with Cheddar cheese. Repeat with chiles, Jack cheese, and optional ham or turkey. Mix egg yolks, flour, and milk. Beat egg whites until stiff and fold in yolk mixture. Pour into pan over cheese. Cover with foil and bake for 1 hour. At this point casserole may be cooled and refrigerated, covered, overnight. Uncover, pour salsa over, and bake another 1/2 hour (40 minutes if refrigerated).

Serves 4-6

Cashew Curry Chicken Salad

6 boneless, skinless chicken breast halves
1/2 teaspoon seasoned salt
1/2 cup cashew halves
1 cup red seedless grapes, halved
3 stalks celery, thinly sliced
2 tablespoons fresh cilantro, chopped
1/2 teaspoon lime juice
1 cup plain nonfat yogurt
2 tablespoons sour cream
1-1/2 teaspoons curry powder
Salt and black pepper to taste

Place chicken in a saucepan with enough water to cover. Add seasoned salt. Bring to boil and simmer, covered, for 15 minutes or until chicken is tender. Remove from pan and cool. Cut chicken into bite-sized pieces. In a large bowl combine the cilantro, lime juice, yogurt, sour cream, and curry powder. Stir in the chicken and celery until well coated with dressing. Gently fold in the grapes halves. Chill the salad. Just before serving, stir in the cashew halves. Season to taste with salt and pepper.

Serves 8

Queen of Hearts

2 sheets frozen puff pastry (12 ounce)
1 egg
2 teaspoons milk
1/2 cup strawberries
1 egg white
1/4 cup powdered sugar
1 teaspoon lemon juice
1/4 cup heavy cream
Strawberry slices
Powdered sugar

Thaw frozen puff pastry for 20 minutes. Cut out eighteen medium sized hearts with a cookie cutter. Whisk together egg and milk to make an egg wash. Lay out six hearts and brush them with egg wash. Top each with another heart. Using a small heart-shaped cookie cutter, cut through the middle of each set of hearts. Remove the smaller hearts, saving one layer. Lay out the remaining six hearts and brush them with egg wash and lay the prepared hearts carefully on top. NOTE: Egg wash needs to be carefully put around edges so the layers stay together. Gently put the saved small heart back into the cut area. Place on cookie sheet, brush with egg wash and bake at 375° for 25-30 minutes or until golden brown. Cool and scoop out the inside of the pastry, leaving the shell.

Puree strawberries and add egg white, powdered sugar, and lemon juice; beat until very thick. Beat 1/4 cup heavy cream and fold into mixture. Fill shells, top with strawberry slices and pastry covers; sprinkle   with powdered sugar.

Serves 6

Apricot Horns

Dough
- 1 pound butter (4 sticks)
- 2 cups creamed cottage cheese (1 pint)
- 4 cups flour

Filling
- 1 pound dried apricots
- 2 cups sugar
- 2 tablespoons almond flavored liqueur (Amaretto)
- 1/2 cup water (variable)

Topping
- 1 egg beaten with 1 teaspoon water
- 1-1/2 cups ground almonds
- 2 cups powdered sugar
- 1/2 teaspoon almond extract
- 1/4 cup light cream (variable)
- Sliced almonds

Preheat oven 375°. Cut the butter into medium sized chunks and place in the large bowl of a processor. Add the cottage cheese and process briefly to blend well. Remove to another bowl and add the flour, mixing well. Shape into 1 inch balls, cover, and refrigerate. (Dough may be kept tightly sealed in the refrigerator for up to 3 weeks.)

Cook the apricots with water (adding small amounts more if they dry out) until tender. There should be very little liquid left. Puree the cooked apricots in the processor, add the sugar, water, and liqueur, mix well, and set aside to cool.

Flatten each ball of dough into a 3 inch round. Work with no more than 10 at a time, keeping the remainder chilled. Place 1 teaspoon of the cold filling in the center and roll into the shape of a horn. Place on a greased cookie sheet and brush the tops with the beaten egg. Sprinkle the ground almonds into the top opening of the horns. Bake 12 to 15 minutes or until lightly browned. Place on rack to cool.

Make an icing by blending the powdered sugar and almond extract with the cream. Add the cream slowly until the proper consistency is reached. The icing should be spreadable—not too thin or too thick.

Ice the still warm horns and decorate with sliced almonds if desired.

Yield 6 to 7 dozen horns

Apple Bars

4 **cups apples, peeled and chopped**
1-1/4 **cups sugar**
2-1/4 **cups flour**
1 **cup butter or margarine**
1/2 **teaspoon salt**
1/2 **teaspoon baking powder**
1 **egg, slightly beaten**
2 **egg yolks, beaten**
1 **teaspoon cinnamon**

Combine 2 cups flour, 1/2 cup sugar, baking, powder, salt. Cut in margarine to pea size; stir in egg yolks. Divide in half and press one half into baking pan.

Combine apples, rest of sugar, flour, cinnamon. Spread over crust. Crumble the rest of the dough over the top and brush with the egg. Bake at 350° until brown. Cool and cut into bars.

Baking time: 13 x 9 x 2-inch pan 40-45 minutes, 15 x 10 x 1-inch pan 35-40 minutes.

Riviera Peach Cake

6 medium sized fresh peaches, peeled, pitted, and sliced
2 large eggs
1-1/2 cups granulated sugar
2 teaspoons hot water
2/3 cup cake flour (or all purpose)
1 teaspoon baking powder
1 teaspoon vanilla extract

Preheat oven to 350°. (325° if using glass baking dish.) In large mixing bowl, beat the eggs with a fork. Add sugar and hot water. Sift flour and baking powder. Add to egg mixture. Mix well. Add vanilla. Mix well. Pour batter into a shallow baking pan. Cover with peaches. Bake for 45 minutes and serve warm.

Blueberry White Chocolate Cake

Cake
1 8-ounce package cream cheese
1 cup sugar
1 teaspoon vanilla
2 large eggs
1-1/2 cups flour
2 teaspoons baking powder
2 cups fresh or frozen blueberries (thawed and rinsed)
1/2 cup coarsely chopped white chocolate
Crust
2 cups graham cracker crumbs
1/4 cup sugar
1/2 teaspoon cinnamon
6 teaspoons melted butter or margarine

Preheat oven to 350°. Mix all crust ingredients together. Pat in bottom of 9-inch square pan. Bake 5 minutes.

Beat cream cheese, sugar and vanilla until fluffy. Beat in eggs, baking powder, and flour thoroughly. Stir on berries and chocolate. Spread batter over baked crust. Bake at 350° for 50-60 minutes or until tester comes out clean. Cool. Dust with powdered sugar before serving.

Sour Lemon Loaf Cake

1-1/3 cups butter
1 cup plus 2 tablespoons granulated sugar
5 large eggs
1 tablespoon lemon zest (yellow skin only, no white)
2 teaspoons baking powder
2 cups cake flour (or all purpose)
1 pinch salt (optional)
1/2 cup lemon juice, freshly squeezed
3/4 cup powdered sugar

Preheat oven to 350° and butter a standard 8 x 5 x 5-inch loaf pan. Cream butter and sugar together until fluffy and light. Beat in eggs one at a time, beating well after each addition.

Add the zest, baking powder, flour and salt (optional) and beat until smooth. Pour batter into prepared loaf pan and bake for 50-60 minutes or until toothpick inserted in center comes up clean.

Cool cake in pan for 10 minutes.

Poke many holes in cake with an ice pick or knitting needle. Blend lemon juice and powdered sugar well and pour over cake. Let cake cool completely before removing from pan. Sprinkle with powdered sugar and slice to serve.

Yield 1 loaf

Desserts

Meringue, Strawberries, Chocolate, and Cream

1/2 cup egg whites (approximately 4 large eggs)
1/4 teaspoon cream of tartar
1 cup granulated sugar
6 ounces semi-sweet chocolate pieces
3 tablespoons water
3 cups heavy (whipping) cream
1/4 cup granulated sugar
1/2 teaspoon vanilla extract
2 pints strawberries (2 baskets)

Preheat oven to 250°. Line baking sheets with waxed paper and on the paper, trace three circles, each 8 inches in diameter.

Beat egg whites until very frothy. Add cream of tartar and beat to distribute. Continue beating and gradually add the sugar. Beat until the meringue is stiff and glossy.

Spread the meringue evenly over the circles, about 1/4 inch thick, and bake in a slow oven for 20-35 minutes, or until meringue is lightly golden. Turn control to off and let the meringues cool in oven. When totally cooled (about 2 hours) remove waxed paper carefully. (Use a spatula to help loosen the meringues.) Wash and drain the strawberries. Reserve a few perfect ones to use as garnish. Remove stems and slice (the long way) the berries. Set aside.

Melt chocolate and water together in top of a double boiler or in the microwave. The consistency will be a little thicker than chocolate syrup. Whip the 3 cups of cream until stiff. Gradually add the 1/4 cup sugar, then the vanilla, and beat until quite stiff.

Place a meringue layer in the center of a serving plate. (Be sure to reserve the prettiest layer for the top.) Spread with a thin coating of melted chocolate (1/3 of chocolate mixture). Then spread a layer about 3/4 inch thick with whipped cream. Top the cream with a layer of sliced strawberries. Place a second meringue layer atop the strawberry layer. Spread with chocolate, another layer of cream, and strawberries.

Top with the prettiest meringue. Cover the sides of the creation smoothly with the remaining whipped cream. Decorate top meringue layer in an informal pattern using remaining melted chocolate squeezed through a pastry cone with a tiny round opening.

Use reserved strawberries to decorate the platter or the top of the dessert. Mint sprigs are a pretty addition also. Chill for a few hours before serving.

Serves 8-10

Torta de Cielo

1/2 pound slivered almonds
1-1/3 cups sugar
6 eggs, separated
Pinch salt
1 tablespoon flour
1 tablespoon Amaretto
1/4 teaspoon cream of tartar
1/2 teaspoon almond extract
4-6 coarsely chopped slivered almonds

Preheat oven to 350°. Grease a 9-1/2 inch springform pan. Line bottom with waxed paper, and grease the paper.

In a blender or food processor, grind almonds with 2/3 cup sugar until very fine, almost a paste. In a large bowl, beat egg yolks, remaining 2/3 cup sugar, and salt until light and creamy. Beat in flour, then Amaretto and almond extract. Beat in almond mixture.

In a large bowl, beat egg whites with cream of tartar until stiff. Fold 1/3 of the egg whites into the nut mixture, then fold in remaining egg whites lightly but thoroughly. Pour into prepared pan. Bake 35 minutes or until browned and cake has begun to shrink from sides of pan. Cake will rise as it bakes, begin to settle in the center and settle even further as it cools. Cool in pan on a rack.

When torte is completely cool, run a knife around the pan to loosen. Remove from pan and decorate with coarsely chopped slivered almonds before serving.

Serves 8

Chocolate Imperiale

Cake
- 3/4 cup semi-sweet chocolate chips
- 4 ounces sweet butter
- 2/3 cup sugar
- Zest of 1 medium orange
- 1 tablespoon Grand Marnier
- 3 large eggs
- 1 cup walnuts, finely ground

Glaze
- 1/2 cup semi-sweet chocolate chips
- 3 ounces sweet butter
- 3 teaspoons light corn syrup

Preheat oven to 375°. Grease and flour an 8-inch springform pan. Line bottom with greased and floured waxed paper.

Melt chocolate and butter in top of double boiler over low heat. Add sugar while the chocolate mixture is still warm. Add the orange zest and transfer mixture to a mixing bowl. Cool for 5 minutes. Stir in the Grand Marnier. Stir in the eggs, one at a time, mixing thoroughly, but do not beat. Stir in the nuts. Pour into the prepared pan. Bake for 30 minutes. Cool completely before removing sides of pan. When cool, invert on a serving platter and remove the waxed paper.

For the glaze, melt the chocolate and butter in top of double boiler. Stir in corn syrup. Pour over the top of cooled cake. Let set a couple of hours. Decorate with fresh mint leaves or berries.

Serves 10-12

Dark 'n' Devilish Cake

1 cup buttermilk
1 cup salad oil
2 large eggs
1 tablespoon vanilla
2 cups flour
2 cups sugar
3/4 cup unsweetened cocoa powder
1 tablespoon baking soda
1 cup boiling water

Preheat oven to 350°. Grease and flour three 8-inch cake pans.

Mix together the buttermilk, oil, eggs and vanilla. Add the sugar and mix well. Sift together the flour, cocoa powder and soda. Add to the buttermilk mixture and beat 2 minutes at medium speed. Add the boiling water and mix to combine. Mixture will be thin. Pour batter into three pans. Bake 35-45 minutes. Let cool in pans for 5 minutes, then invert onto cooling racks.

When completely cool, frost with chocolate cream cheese frosting.

Chocolate Cream Cheese Frosting

1 8-ounce package cream cheese, room temperature
1/2 cup butter or margarine, room temperature
1-1/2 cups powdered sugar
4-6 tablespoons milk or enough for desired consistency
2 squares unsweetened chocolate, melted

Cream together the cream cheese and butter. Add sugar, chocolate and milk until spreadable consistency.

Serves 8-12

Coconut Cake

Cake
- 1/2 cup butter or margarine
- 1/2 cup shortening
- 2 cups sugar
- 5 eggs, room temperature
- 2 cups flour
- 1 teaspoon baking soda
- 1 cup buttermilk
- 1 teaspoon vanilla
- 1 7-ounce package flaked coconut
- 1/4 cup pecans or walnuts, chopped

Frosting
- 1 8-ounce package cream cheese, room temperature
- 1/2 cup butter or margarine, room temperature
- 1 box powdered sugar
- 1 teaspoon vanilla
- 1/4 cup nuts
- 1/4 cup coconut, toasted

Preheat oven to 350°. Grease and flour three 8-inch cake pans.

Cream together butter, shortening, and sugar until light and fluffy. Add eggs one at a time making sure to beat well after each addition. Add flour, soda, buttermilk, and vanilla, and mix thoroughly. Add coconut and nuts. Pour evenly into three prepared cake pans. Bake 29 minutes exactly. Do not overcook. Let cool in pans 5 minutes before turning out to cooling racks. Cool completely before frosting.

Beat cream cheese and butter together until fluffy. Add powdered sugar and vanilla. Beat well. Frost tops and sides and assemble three layers, garnishing top layer with nuts and toasted coconut.

Serves 8-12

Triple Decker Chocolate-Rum Cake

First Layer Ingredients
- 1-1/2 cups cake flour
- 1 cup granulated sugar
- 1-1/2 teaspoons baking powder
- 1 teaspoon baking soda
- 4 tablespoons cocoa
- 1/2 teaspoon salt (optional)
- 1/2 cup water
- 1/2 cup rum
- 1 cup mayonnaise

First Layer Directions: Preheat oven to 350°. Generously butter a springform pan.

Sift together the cake flour, sugar, baking powder, baking soda, cocoa, and salt (optional). Set aside. In a separate bowl, mix the water, rum and mayonnaise well, and add to the sifted dry ingredients. Pour mixture into the prepared pan. Bake at 350° for 30 minutes. Cool IN PAN (do not remove from pan until you are ready to do third layer) for 2-3 hours.

Second Layer Ingredients
- 1-1/2 teaspoon rum flavoring
- 12 ounce package chocolate chips
- 8 large eggs, separated

Second Layer Directions: Melt chocolate chips with 2 tablespoons water in top of double boiler. Let cool and add rum flavoring. Beat egg yolks and blend with chocolate until smooth. Being sure that mixer blades are clean, beat egg whites until stiff but still shiny, and fold carefully into chocolate-egg mixture. Pour this mixture over first cake layer in springform pan. Refrigerate at least 3 hours.

Third Layer Ingredients
   1-1/2 cups heavy (whipping) cream
   2 tablespoons powdered sugar
   2 teaspoons rum

Third Layer Directions: Whip cream until it forms peaks. Add sugar gradually as you continue beating. Add rum and beat to incorporate. Carefully loosen cake from the sides of the springform pan. Remove cake from pan to serving platter. Spread whipped cream on sides and top of cake. Sprinkle top with grated chocolate.

Serves 10

Pumpkin Roulé

Cake
- 3 eggs
- 1 cup sugar
- 2/3 cup canned pumpkin
- 1 teaspoon lemon juice
- 3/4 cup flour
- 1 teaspoon baking powder
- 2 teaspoons cinnamon
- 1 teaspoon ginger
- 1/2 teaspoon nutmeg
- Roule filling (see below)

Preheat oven to 350°. Grease and flour jelly roll pan (10-1/2 x 15-inches).

Beat the eggs for 5 minutes. Add the sugar, pumpkin, and lemon juice and mix well. Add the dry ingredients and mix thoroughly. Spread pumpkin mixture evenly into prepared pan. Bake for 12-15 minutes or until cake springs back when lightly touched. Turn hot cake out onto a non-terry cloth towel sprinkled with sifted powdered sugar. Immediately roll up cake starting with 10-1/2 inch side and keep the cake rolled until cool. Unroll to fill.

Roulé filling
- 1 3-ounce package cream cheese, room temperature
- 1 cup powdered sugar
- 2-3 tablespoons milk
- 1/4 cup butter or margarine, room temperature
- 1/4 teaspoon maple extract

Beat cream cheese and butter together until fluffy. Add powdered sugar and enough milk to make the filling spreadable. Add the maple extract and spread on cooled cake, making sure not to put filling too close to the edges. Once filled, re-roll and refrigerate until serving time. Dust with powdered sugar and slice with serrated knife.

Serves 8-10

Walnut Roulé

Cake
- **7 eggs, separated**
- **3/4 cup sugar**
- **1 teaspoon vanilla**
- **1 teaspoon baking powder**
- **1 tablespoon (heaping) flour**
- **1 cup walnuts, finely chopped**

Filling
- **1 cup whipping cream**
- **2-3 tablespoons sugar or sweetened to taste**

Preheat oven to 350°. Grease a jelly roll pan (10-1/2 x 15-inches), line with wax paper. Grease and flour paper.

Beat egg yolks, sugar, and vanilla until well blended. Add dry ingredients and beat until ribbony yellow. Add nuts and mix well.

Beat egg whites until stiff. Fold whites into nut mixture. Pour batter into pan. Bake for 15 minutes or until cake springs back when lightly touched.

Turn hot cake out onto non-terry cloth towel sprinkled with sifted powdered sugar. Immediately remove wax paper. Roll up cake starting with 10-1/2 inch side and keep rolled until cool. Unroll to fill.

Beat whipping cream until soft peaks form. Add sugar to taste and beat until stiff peaks form. Spread evenly over cake making sure filling is not too close to the edges. Re-roll and refrigerate until serving time. Dust with sifted powdered sugar and slice with serrated knife.

Serves 8-10

Amaretto Cheesecake

Crust
- 1-1/2 cups chocolate wafer crumbs
  (not filled chocolate cookies)
- 1 cup blanched almonds, lightly toasted and finely chopped
- 1/3 cup granulated sugar
- 6 tablespoons butter, melted
- 3 8-ounce packages cream cheese, at room temperature
- 1 cup granulated sugar
- 4 large eggs
- 1/3 cup heavy (whipping) cream
- 1/4 cup (plus) almond-flavored liqueur such as Amaretto
- 1/2 teaspoon vanilla extract
- 1/2 teaspoon almond extract

Topping
- 1 pint (2 cups) sour cream
- 1 tablespoon granulated sugar
- 1 teaspoon vanilla extract

Garnish
- Slivered, blanched almonds

Butter a 9-1/2 inch springform pan. Preheat oven to 375°. Combine the chocolate wafer crumbs, 1 cup chopped almonds, 1/3 cup sugar and 3/4 stick melted butter. Pat into the bottom and up the sides of the prepared pan.

In a large mixing bowl, cream together the cream cheese and 1 cup sugar. Add the eggs, one at a time, beating well after each addition. Add 1/3 cup cream, 1/4 cup (plus) almond-flavored liqueur, 1/2 teaspoon vanilla and 1/2 teaspoon almond extract. Beat the mixture until it is light. Pour the batter into the crust and bake, in the center of the oven, for 35 minutes. Transfer cake to a wire rack and let stand for 5 minutes. (The cake will NOT be set.)

In a small mixing bowl, combine the 2 cups sour cream, 1 tablespoon sugar, and 1 teaspoon vanilla well. Spread the mixture evenly over the cake and bake for 5 minutes more. Transfer cake to the wire rack and cool completely. Cover lightly with plastic wrap and refrigerate overnight.

To serve, remove sides of pan, transfer cake to serving platter and garnish with blanched, slivered almonds.

Serves 10-12

Coconut Cheesecake

>   3 8-ounce packages cream cheese, room temperature
>   1-1/2 cups sugar
>   4 large eggs, room temperature
>   2 egg yolks, room temperature
>   2 cups flaked coconut
>   1 cup whipping cream
>   1 teaspoon fresh lemon juice
>   1/2 teaspoon vanilla
>   1/2 teaspoon almond extract

Topping
>   1 cup toasted coconut

Crust
>   1-1/2 cups graham cracker crumbs, finely crushed
>   1/3 cup sugar
>   1/3-1/2 cup butter or margarine, melted

Preheat oven to 300°. Spray a 9-1/2 inch springform pan with non-stick cooking spray. Combine all crust ingredients and press into bottom of pan.

Beat cream cheese and sugar until light and fluffy. Beat in eggs and yolks one at a time. Beat in coconut, whipping cream, lemon juice, and extracts until thoroughly mixed. Pour into pan. Bake about 70 minutes or until edges of filling are firm. Let cool completely. Refrigerate at least 4 hours before serving. Top with toasted coconut.

Serves 12

Pumpkin Cheesecake

2 8-ounce packages cream cheese
1 cup sugar
3 eggs
1 tablespoon flour
2 teaspoons cinnamon
1 teaspoon ginger
1 1-pound can pumpkin
2 tablespoons rum

Topping
1 cup whipping cream
3 tablespoons sugar
1/2 teaspoon cinnamon

Crust
3/4 cup graham cracker crumbs
3/4 cup finely crushed gingersnap cookies
1/3 cup butter or margarine, melted

Preheat oven to 350°. Spray a 9-inch springform pan with non-stick cooking spray. Combine graham cracker and gingersnap cookie crumbs with melted butter or margarine. Press on sides and bottom of pan. Bake 8 minutes. Reduce oven temperature to 300°.

Beat cream cheese until fluffy. Gradually beat in sugar. Add eggs one at a time, beating after each. Mix in flour, cinnamon, and ginger. Stir in pumpkin and rum. Pour into baked crust. Bake for 1-1/2 hours, or until center feels firm. Turn off oven, open oven door slightly and leave cheesecake in for an additional hour. Cool completely. Refrigerate.

Whip cream until stiff peaks form, add sugar and cinnamon. To serve, top each slice with a dollop of spiced whipped cream.

Serves 12

Turtles

1 cup flour
1 cup quick oats
1/4 teaspoon salt (optional)
1/2 teaspoon baking soda
3/4 cup brown sugar
3/4 cup melted butter or margarine
1 cup semi-sweet chocolate chips
1-1/2 cups chopped pecans
32 caramel candies, unwrapped
5 tablespoons cream

Preheat oven to 350°. Set aside an ungreased 7 x 11-inch baking pan.

Mix together the flour, oatmeal, salt, soda, brown sugar, and melted butter or margarine. Pat half of the mixture into the pan and bake 10 minutes. While the base is baking, begin to melt the caramels and cream over a double boiler. Remove the base from the oven and sprinkle with the chocolate chips and pecans. Pour melted caramels over chips and nuts and spread remaining half of crumb mixture over the top. Bake 15-20 minutes more. Let cool completely before cutting into squares.

Yield 28 squares

Note: 1-1/2 recipe will fill a 9 x 13-inch pan.

Lemon Soufflé Cheesecake

1 envelope plain gelatin
3/4 cup plus 1 tablespoon fresh lemon juice
1-1/2 cups sugar
4 eggs, room temperature
2 egg yolks, room temperature
2 tablespoons grated lemon peel
2 8-ounce packages cream cheese, room temperature
1/2 cup unsalted butter, room temperature
3 drops yellow food color
2 egg whites, room temperature
1/8 teaspoon salt
Pinch of cream of tartar
1/4 cup sugar
Crust
1-1/2 cups finely crushed graham crackers
1/3 cup brown sugar
1/3-1/2 cup butter or margarine, melted
Topping
Sliced fresh seasonal fruit, such as kiwi, strawberries,
raspberries or blueberries

Spray a 9-1/2 inch springform pan with non-stick cooking spray.
Combine all crust ingredients and press onto bottom of pan.

Soften gelatin in lemon juice for 5 minutes in a medium saucepan.
Add 1-1/2 cups sugar, whole eggs, yolks, and lemon peel. Stir to mix.
Cook over medium heat until it is the consistency of loose pudding,
about 7 minutes. Beat cream cheese and butter until smooth.
Gradually beat in hot lemon custard. Mix in food coloring. Cool 15
minutes. Refrigerate for 30 minutes, stirring occasionally.

Beat egg whites with salt and cream of tartar. Add sugar gradually
and beat until stiff. Fold egg whites into refrigerated mixture. Pour
into crust and refrigerate at least 8 hours before serving.

Before serving, top with fresh seasonal fruit.

Serves 12

Toffee Bars

1 cup butter or margarine, softened
1 cup brown sugar
2 cups flour
4 eggs
2 cups brown sugar
2 teaspoons vanilla
4 tablespoons flour
2 teaspoons baking powder
1 14-ounce package shredded coconut
2-1/4 cups chopped pecans

Preheat oven to 350°. Spray a 12 x 16-inch baking pan with non-stick cooking spray.

Beat butter or margarine and 1 cup brown sugar together until light and fluffy. Add 2 cups flour and mix well. Press mixture down by hand in pan. Bake 10 minutes.

Beat eggs well. Add 2 cups brown sugar and vanilla and mix thoroughly. Stir in 4 tablespoons flour and baking powder. When mixed, add coconut and pecans. When mixture is thoroughly stirred, spread on bottom layer and bake an additional 25 minutes.

These toffee bars are very rich and delicious. They freeze very well, so can be made ahead for any occasion.

Yield 70 bars

Chocolate Mint Brownies

Brownies
  2 ounces unsweetened chocolate
  1/2 cup butter or margarine
  2 eggs
  1 cup sugar
  1/2 cup flour
  1/2 cup chopped pecans or walnuts
Mint cream
  1-1/2 cups powdered sugar
  3 tablespoons soft butter or margarine
  2 tablespoons milk
  3/4 teaspoon peppermint extract
Chocolate glaze
  2 ounces semi-sweet chocolate
  2 tablespoons butter or margarine

Preheat oven to 350°. Grease a 9-inch square pan.

Brownies: Melt chocolate and butter together over double boiler or in microwave. Cool. Beat together the eggs and sugar until ivory colored. Add flour and nuts and mix well. Add chocolate-butter mixture and mix thoroughly. Pour into prepared pan. Bake 25 minutes. Cool.

Mint cream: Beat all ingredients together until smooth. Spread over cooled brownies. Cover and chill until firm, about 1 hour.

Chocolate glaze: Melt chocolate and butter over double boiler or in microwave. Spread over chilled, frosted brownies. Chill until firm.

Yield 36 brownies

White Chocolate Macadamia Nut Brownies

2 large eggs, room temperature
1/2 cup sugar
7 ounces imported white chocolate
1/2 cup unsalted butter
1 cup flour
1 teaspoon vanilla
1 cup chopped macadamia nuts*
5 ounces imported white chocolate, coarsely chopped

*If salted, rinse under hot water, drain and dry thoroughly before chopping.

Spray a 7 x 11-inch pan with non-stick cooking spray.

With a mixer, beat eggs until frothy. Add sugar, 1 tablespoonful at a time, and beat until a pale yellow ribbon forms. Add flour and vanilla. Mix well.

Melt the 7 ounces of white chocolate and butter over a double boiler. Mixture may look curdled and will not mix together well. Fold in chocolate-butter mixture and mix thoroughly. Fold in nuts and chopped 5 ounces white chocolate. Pour into pan. Bake approximately 25 minutes or until a toothpick comes out clean. DO NOT OVERBAKE. Cool and frost with chocolate cream cheese frosting.

Frosting
1 3-ounce package cream cheese, room temperature
1/4 cup butter, room temperature
1-1/4 cups powdered sugar
1 ounce unsweetened chocolate, melted

Mix all ingredients together thoroughly. Spread on cooled brownies.

Yield 8 brownies

Chocolate Macaroons

1 4-ounce German sweet chocolate
1 1-ounce square unsweetened chocolate
2 egg whites, room temperature
Pinch salt
1/2 cup sugar
1 teaspoon vanilla
1 7-ounce package coconut

Preheat oven to 325°. Spray cookie sheets with non-stick cooking spray.

Melt two chocolates in a double boiler over moderate heat. Cover until almost melted. Uncover and stir until smooth. Remove and cool to room temperature.

Beat egg whites with salt until stiff peaks form. Add sugar a few tablespoonfuls at a time. Add vanilla. Increase speed on mixer to high and beat 5 minutes. Reduce mixer speed to low. Add chocolates and beat only until mixed. Fold in coconut. Spoon tablespoonfuls of batter onto cookie sheets, placing each 1-2 inches apart. Bake 16-20 minutes or until they feel dry on the outside, soft in the center. Remove macaroons from cookie sheets and cool on racks.

Yield 16 cookies

Oatmeal Chocolate Chip Cookies

1-1/2 cups sugar
1 pound margarine, softened
1-1/2 cups brown sugar
3 eggs
1/2 teaspoon salt
1/2 teaspoon baking soda
6 cups old-fashioned oats
1 cup chocolate chips
1 cup coconut
1 cup chopped nuts
2 cups whole wheat flour

Preheat oven to 325°.

Cream together the margarine and sugars in a very large mixing bowl. Add eggs and beat thoroughly. Fold in the remaining ingredients in the following order: chocolate chips, coconut, nuts, oats, flour, salt, and soda.

Place by heaping tablespoonfuls onto ungreased cookie sheets. Bake for 12 minutes or until lightly browned.

Yield 6 dozen cookies; recipe may be halved

White Chocolate Chip Cookies

1-1/2 pounds butter, room temperature
1-1/2 cups sugar
3 cups brown sugar
6 eggs
1 tablespoon vanilla
6-3/4 cups flour
1 tablespoon baking soda
4 cups white chocolate chips
2 cups coconut
2 cups pecans, coarsely chopped

Preheat oven to 350°.

Beat butter with sugars until smooth. Add eggs one at a time. Add vanilla. Sift flour with soda and add to batter. Mix thoroughly. Add chips, coconut, and nuts. Roll dough into small walnut-sized balls and place on cookie sheets sprayed with non-stick cooking spray.

Bake for 8-12 minutes.

Yield 10 dozen cookies; recipe may be halved

Almond Apricot Bars

Cake
  1 7-ounce tube of almond paste
  3/4 cup plus 1 tablespoon sugar
  7 tablespoons butter or margarine, softened
  3 eggs
  1/2 cup sifted cake flour
Crust
  1 cup flour
  1/2 cup butter or margarine
  1/4 cup powdered sugar
Topping
  2 8-1/4 ounce cans of apricot halves, drained
     (approximately 12 halves)
  1 cup sliced almonds

Preheat oven to 350°. Spray 9-inch square pan with non-stick cooking spray.

Mix crust ingredients together in food processor. Press into bottom of pan. Bake 20 minutes.

While crust is baking, in food processor mix almond paste, sugar, and butter together. Add eggs one at a time. Add flour and blend with one or two on/off switches.

Pour cake batter on top of hot crust. Place apricot halves on top. Sprinkle with sliced almonds. Bake for additional 40-50 minutes or until toothpick inserted in center comes out clean.

Yield 12

Lemon Cheesecake Bars

5 tablespoons butter or margarine
1/2 cup brown sugar
1 cup flour
1/2 cup chopped nuts
1/2 cup sugar
1 8-ounce package cream cheese
1 egg
2 tablespoons milk
1 tablespoon lemon juice
1/4 teaspoon vanilla

Preheat oven to 350°. Spray 8-inch square pan with non-stick cooking spray.

Cream butter and brown sugar together. Add nuts and flour and mix thoroughly. Set aside 1 cup of this mixture for topping. Press remainder in pan. Bake for 12-15 minutes or until golden brown.

Blend sugar and cream cheese until smooth. Add egg, milk, lemon juice, and vanilla. Beat well. Spread over baked crust. Sprinkle with 1 cup of topping. Return to oven and bake for an additional 25 minutes. Cool. Chill in refrigerator at least 2 hours. Cut into squares; depending on cut size, makes 15-30 squares. This recipe can be doubled for a 9 x 13-inch pan. Bake for an additional 10-15 minutes. Depending on cut size, makes 30-48 squares.

Yield for 8-inch pan— 15-30 squares; 9 x 13-inch pan—30-48 squares

Apricot Chocolate Torte

Crust
    1/2 box chocolate wafer cookies (about 20 cookies),
           finely crushed
    3 tablespoons butter or margarine, melted

Filling
    4 eggs
    1 teaspoon baking powder
    2 teaspoons vanilla
    1-1/2 cups walnuts, finely chopped
    1 cup dried apricots, chopped

Glaze
    6 tablespoons semi-sweet chocolate chips
    1/2 ounce unsweetened chocolate (1/2 square)
    5 tablespoons butter or margarine

Preheat oven to 350°. Spray 8-inch round pan with non-stick cooking spray.

Crust: Combine crushed cookies with melted butter or margarine with a fork. Press onto bottom of pan and bake for 8 minutes.

Filling: Beat eggs until slightly thick. Stir in baking powder, vanilla, nuts, and apricots. Pour over baked crust. Bake 20 minutes. Cool before glazing.

Glaze: Place glaze ingredients in glass dish and heat in microwave just until melted. Stir to combine all ingredients. Pour over top and smooth to cover top completely. Let set for about 2 hours before serving.

Serves 8

Lemon Mousse

6 tablespoons butter
3 eggs
2/3 cup sugar
1/2 cup fresh lemon juice
1-1/2 cups whipping cream
Zest of one lemon
1 cup of fresh berries (blueberries, raspberries, blackberries,
     or sliced strawberries)

In a double boiler, melt butter. In a bowl, beat eggs and sugar until foamy. Add melted butter and lemon juice. Cook mixture in a double boiler until it becomes a custard-like consistency, about 5 minutes on medium-low heat. Remove from heat and chill.

Whip cream until stiff. Fold in cream and zest and then carefully fold in the berries. Ladle mixture into chilled custard cups. Chill several hours before serving.

Serves 6-8

Macadamia Nut Chocolate Mousse Pie

1 8-ounce package cream cheese, room temperature
1/3 cup sugar
1 teaspoon vanilla
2 eggs, separated, room temperature
1 cup semi-sweet chocolate chips, melted
Pinch cream of tartar
1/3 cup sugar
1 cup whipping cream, well-chilled
1-1/2 cups macadamia nuts, chopped*
Crust
1 cup graham cracker crumbs
1/4 cup butter or margarine, melted
Topping
1 cup whipping cream, well-chilled
2 tablespoons powdered sugar
Garnish
Chocolate curls or chocolate leaves

*If salted, rinse under hot water, drain and dry thoroughly
 before chopping

Preheat oven to 350°. Spray 9-inch pie pan with non-stick cooking spray. Combine crust ingredients and mix thoroughly. Press onto bottom and sides of pan. Bake 5-7 minutes. Cool completely.

Beat cream cheese, 1/3 cup sugar, and vanilla until creamy. Add yolks and beat until smooth. Mix in melted chocolate chips. Using clean dry beaters, beat whites and cream of tartar until soft peaks form. Add 1/3 cup sugar, 1 tablespoon at a time, and heat until stiff peaks form. Gently fold whites into chocolate mixture. Whip 1 cup whipping cream to form firm peaks. Fold cream and nuts into chocolate mixture. Pour into crust. Refrigerate at least 6 hours.

To serve, beat 1 cup whipping cream with powdered sugar to soft peaks. Spread over chocolate mixture and garnish with chocolate curls or chocolate leaves.

Serves 8

Apricot Yogurt Mousse with Raspberry Sauce

1/2 cup dried large apricots (approximately 15)
1/2 cup frozen orange juice concentrate, thawed
1/4 cup cold water
1 tablespoon unflavored gelatin (1 envelope)
4 large egg whites
2/3 cup plus 2 tablespoons sugar, divided
2 tablespoons fresh lemon juice
1-1/2 cups plain yogurt

Sauce
2 14-ounce package frozen raspberries (thawed)
1/3 cup light corn syrup

Garnish
2 seedless oranges, very thinly sliced

Combine apricots and orange juice concentrate in a small saucepan and mix well. Cover and marinate overnight. Place apricot mixture over medium-low heat and cook until apricots are softened, about 10 minutes. Press apricots down into the liquid during cooking time. Remove from heat and set aside.

Pour 1/4 cup cold water into a cup and sprinkle with gelatin. Let stand until all the water is absorbed. Set cup into pan of hot water until gelatin is dissolved. Beat egg whites with 2 tablespoons of sugar until stiff peaks form. Add lemon juice and beat until well mixed. Combine apricots, soaking liquid and remaining 2/3 cup sugar and purée in food processor or blender. Add dissolved gelatin and blend 10 seconds. If gelatin has started to set, warm slightly in hot water before adding. Make sure to scrape all gelatin out of cup.

Add 1/2 cup of yogurt and blend well. Add remaining 1 cup yogurt. Fold in the egg whites. Transfer to large bowl, cover with plastic wrap and refrigerate at least 4 hours.

Sauce: Place thawed raspberries in blender or food processor. While running, add corn syrup. Put mixture through sieve to remove seeds. Put sauce in bowl and refrigerate.

To serve: Layer mousse and sauce in parfait glasses and top with thinly sliced orange. Refrigerate until serving time.

Serves 8-10

Deep Dish Blueberry Pie

Crust
>   1-1/2 cups flour
>   1 cube butter or margarine
>   2 tablespoons sugar
>   1 tablespoon white vinegar

Filling
>   3 cups fresh blueberries
>   1 cup sugar
>   2 tablespoons flour
>   1/2 teaspoon cinnamon

Topping
>   1 cup fresh blueberries

Preheat oven to 375°. Spray 8-inch cake pan with non-stick spray.

Crust: Combine flour and butter until crumbly. Add sugar and white vinegar and mix thoroughly. Mixture will still be crumbly. Press into bottom and sides of pan.

Filling: Combine all filling ingredients. Let set for about 20-30 minutes or until sugar has dissolved. Pour into crust. Bake for one hour at 375°.

Remove from oven and immediately press 1 cup fresh blueberries into the top of the pie.

Serves 8

Cranberry Apple Crisp

   8 large tart green apples, peeled, cored
1-1/3 cups cranberries
  1/3 cup sugar
   2 tablespoons fresh lemon juice
Topping
   1 cup old-fashioned oats
  3/4 cup flour
  3/4 cup brown sugar
1-1/2 teaspoons cinnamon
  1/2 teaspoon nutmeg
   1 cube butter or margarine, softened
  3/4 cup chopped pecans
  1/2 cup raisins

Preheat oven to 375°. Spray 9 x 13-inch pan with non-stick spray.

Slice apples into 1/4 inch thick slices. Combine apples, cranberries, sugar, and lemon juice. Toss carefully. Pour into prepared pan.

Topping: Combine oats, flour, brown sugar, cinnamon, and nutmeg. Add butter and mix until crumbly. Stir in nuts and raisins. Sprinkle over apple-cranberry mixture. Cover with foil. Bake for 20 minutes. Uncover and bake for an additional 40 minutes. Serve warm with vanilla ice cream.

Serves 12

Almond Cake with Raspberry Sauce

3/4 cup sugar
1/2 cup unsalted butter
8 ounces almond paste
3 eggs
2 tablespoons cherry liqueur (Kirsch)
1/4 teaspoon almond extract
1/4 cup flour
1/3 teaspoon baking powder
Powdered sugar for garnish
2 cups fresh raspberries or 12 ounces frozen-thawed
2 tablespoons sugar (or as needed to taste for fresh
    raspberries)

Preheat oven to 350°. Butter and flour a 9 inch round cake pan or springform pan.

In a bowl, combine the sugar, butter, and almond paste. If using an electric mixer, use low speed. Add the eggs, liqueur, and extract and mix well. Combine the flour and baking powder and add all at once, beating until just barely mixed. Do not overbeat. Spread into the prepared pan and bake 40 minutes or until done when tested. (Use a toothpick to pierce the center of the cake. The cake is done if the toothpick comes out clean.) Cool on a wire rack and then invert onto a cake platter. Dust with powdered sugar to garnish.

Puree the raspberries in a blender or food processor, strain, and sweeten to taste. If the sauce is too thin, heat to reduce or add a mixture of 1 tablespoon of cornstarch blended with 1 tablespoon of cold water. Cook and stir until the sauce is thickened.

To serve, ladle the raspberry sauce onto the dessert plate and top with a wedge of the cake.

Serves 8

Blue Ribbon Carrot Cake

2 cups all purpose flour
2 teaspoons baking soda
2 teaspoons cinnamon
1/2 teaspoon salt
3 eggs
3/4 cup oil
3/4 cup buttermilk
1 cup sugar
2 teaspoons vanilla
1 8-ounce can crushed pineapple, drained
2 cups grated carrots
3-1/2 ounces shredded coconut
1 cup chopped walnuts or 1 cup of raisins

Buttermilk Glaze

1 cup sugar
1/2 cup buttermilk
1/2 teaspoon baking soda
1/2 cup butter
1 tablespoon corn syrup
1 teaspoon vanilla

Cream Cheese Frosting

1/2 cup butter
1 8-ounce package cream cheese
1 teaspoon vanilla
2 cups powdered sugar
1 teaspoon orange zest
1 teaspoon orange juice

Preheat oven to 350°. Grease one 9 inch x 13 inch baking pan or two 9-inch layer cake pans.

Sift together the flour, baking soda, cinnamon and salt. Set aside.

In a large bowl, beat the eggs and add the oil, buttermilk, sugar, and vanilla. Mix well. Add the flour mixture and then the pineapple, carrots, coconut, and walnuts or raisins. Stir and mix well. Pour the batter into the prepared baking pan(s) and bake for 50 minutes or until a toothpick inserted into the middle of the cake comes out clean. While the cake is baking, prepare Buttermilk Glaze and Cream Cheese Frosting (see below).

Pour Buttermilk Glaze over the hot cake while in the pan(s).

Allow the glaze to be absorbed thoroughly (about 15 minutes). When cooled completely remove the cake from the pan by running a knife around all edges and invert onto a serving platter.

To prepare Buttermilk Glaze: In a saucepan, combine all the ingredients except the vanilla. Bring to a boil and cook 5 minutes, stirring frequently. Remove from heat and stir in the vanilla.

To prepare Cream Cheese Frosting: Blend the butter and cream cheese together until fluffy. Add the vanilla, powdered sugar, zest, and juice. Mix well to an easy spreading consistency. Add additional sugar or juice as needed.

Frost the cake with Cream Cheese Frosting and chill before serving.

Serves 12—9 x 13-inch pan; 8-10—two 9-inch layer pans

Applesauce Cake with Caramel Icing

4 cups sifted flour
4 teaspoons baking soda
1-1/4 teaspoons salt
2 teaspoons cinnamon
1/2 teaspoon ground cloves
2 tablespoons cocoa
1 cup oil
2 cups sugar
3 cups unsweetened applesauce, heated
1/2 cup raisins
1/2 cup chopped walnuts
Caramel icing (recipe below)

Preheat oven as required (see below). Grease and flour two 9-inch square pans, one 9 x 13-inch baking pan, or one 9-inch bundt or tube pan.

In a large bowl, sift together the flour, baking soda, salt, cinnamon, cloves, and cocoa. In a small bowl, stir the oil and sugar together thoroughly. Add this to the flour mixture and blend. Stir in the hot applesauce. Mix in the raisins and walnuts. Pour into the prepared pan(s) and bake: 375° for two 9-inch pans for 30 minutes or until tested done. 350° for one 9 x 13-inch pan for 35 minutes or until tested done. 325° for one 9-inch bundt or tube pan for 55 minutes or until tested done.

Cool the cake in the pan for 5 minutes before turning out onto a wire rack. Ice when thoroughly cooled.

Serves 20

Caramel Icing

1/2 cup butter or margarine
1 cup brown sugar
1/4 cup milk
2 cups powdered sugar

Melt the butter in a saucepan and add the brown sugar. Bring to a boil and stir constantly while boiling for 2 minutes. Add the milk, beat well, and allow to return to a full boil. Remove from heat and cool to lukewarm. Stir in the powdered sugar and beat with a wire whip until smooth.

This is a generous amount of icing that can be used as a filling between layers as well as for icing the top and sides. For the bundt or tube cake, a swirl of icing just on the top, garnished with walnut halves, makes an attractively finished cake.

Makes approximately 3 cups

White Chocolate Cheesecake with Raspberry Sauce

4 8-ounce packages cream cheese, room temperature
6 ounces white chocolate, finely chopped
5 large eggs
3/4 cup sugar
3 tablespoons flour
1 teaspoon vanilla
1/2 teaspoon almond extract
Topping
   1 14-ounce package frozen raspberries, thawed and drained
   1/3 cup light corn syrup
Crust
   2 cups finely ground shortbread cookie crumbs
   1/2 cup ground almonds, toasted
   3 tablespoons sugar
   3/4 cube butter, melted

Preheat oven to 350°. Combine all crust ingredients. Press on bottom and sides of 10-inch springform pan. Bake 10 minutes. Reduce heat to 325°.

Filling: Melt chocolate in top of double boiler over hot but not boiling water, cool. Beat cheese, 1/2 cup sugar, vanilla, and almond extract until smooth. Beat in eggs one at a time. Mix flour and remaining 1/4 cup sugar, add to cheese mixture and beat until incorporated. Stir 1 cup of mixture into cooled chocolate. Mix in remaining filling. Pour filling over crust. Bake for 45 minutes or until center of filling moves slightly when side of pan is tapped. Cool and refrigerate.

Topping: Purée raspberries in food processor, slowly add corn syrup. Press through sieve to remove seeds. Refrigerate until serving time. To serve spoon a tablespoon of topping over each slice.

Serves 12

Index

Notes

Notes

A Slice of Santa Barbara

Mail To: JLSB Cookbook
P.O. Box 90645
Santa Barbara, CA 93190-0645

Please send me ____copies of *A Slice of Santa Barbara* at $15.95 per book plus $2.50 for postage and handling per book. Enclosed you will find my check or money order for $_____ .

Make checks payable to: JLSB, Cookbook—California residents add 7.75% sales tax.

Name _____

Address _____

_____

City _____ State _____ Zip _____

Please send me ____copies of *A Slice of Santa Barbara* at $15.95 per book plus $2.50 for postage and handling per book. Enclosed you will find my check or money order for $_____ .

Make checks payable to: JLSB, Cookbook—California residents add 7.75% sales tax.

Name _____

Address _____

_____

City _____ State _____ Zip _____

Please send me ____copies of *A Slice of Santa Barbara* at $15.95 per book plus $2.50 for postage and handling per book. Enclosed you will find my check or money order for $_____ .

Make checks payable to: JLSB, Cookbook—California residents add 7.75% sales tax.

Name _____

Address _____

_____

City _____ State _____ Zip _____